A Livy Reader
Selections from
Ab Urbe Condita

Mary Jaeger

Bolchazy-Carducci Publishers, Inc.
Mundelein, Illinois USA

𝄞 LATIN Readers

These readers provide well annotated Latin selections written by experts in the field, to be used as authoritative introductions to Latin authors, genres, topics, or themes for intermediate or advanced college Latin study. Their relatively small size (covering 500–600 lines) makes them ideal to use in combination. Each volume includes a comprehensive introduction, bibliography for further reading, Latin text with notes at the back, and complete vocabulary. Nineteen volumes are currently scheduled for publication; others are under consideration. Check our website for updates: www.BOLCHAZY.com.

Series Editor: Ronnie Ancona

Volume Editor: Laurie Haight Keenan

Cover Design & Typography: Adam Phillip Velez

Maps: Mapping Specialists, Ltd.

A Livy Reader
Selections from Ab Urbe Condita

Mary Jaeger

Bolchazy-Carducci Publishers, Inc.
1570 Baskin Road
Mundelein, Illinois 60060
www.bolchazy.com

Printed in the United States of America
2011
by United Graphics

ISBN 978-0-86516-680-6

Library of Congress Cataloging-in-Publication Data

Livy.
 [Ab urbe condita. English. Selections]
 A Livy reader : selections from Ab urbe condita / Mary Jaeger.
     p. cm. -- (BC latin readers)
 Includes bibliographical references and index.
 ISBN 978-0-86516-680-6 (pbk. : alk. paper)
 I. Jaeger, Mary, 1960- II. Title.
 PA6452.A3J34 2011
 937.01--dc22

                                                                  2010048897

Contents

List of Illustrations

Preface

Writing a commentary on some 600 lines of Livy is a process both pleasant and frustrating: one has the opportunity to reread favorite passages of Livy closely; but from the hundreds of fascinating narratives in the surviving portion of the *Ab Urbe Condita*, which to choose? Once the passages have been selected, others equally worthy come to mind. To include the stories of Horatius, Mucius Scaevola, and Cloelia means excluding those of Tanaquil, the Tarquins, and Lucretia; including Hannibal's first speech means leaving out Camillus' praise of Rome; including the crossing of the Alps means leaving out the fall of Syracuse. Including Cannae (and only its immediate aftermath, at that) means excluding the Caudine Forks, and Nola, and so on. Rome's early history is rich in incident; and the surviving books of the *Ab Urbe Condita* provide the commentator with an embarrassment of such wealth.

Because this volume will be its users' first, and for many their only, exposure to Livy, I have tried to give a representative sample of passages, one which illustrates Livy's versatility as a writer, and most of all, his excellence as a storyteller. This selection will, I hope, encourage students to make a more extensive exploration of Livy's text. For those wishing to do so, there are many excellent English-language commentaries on the specific books. The Bibliography contains a list of those, several of which I have consulted in composing this volume. Because of the nature of commentary writing, it was occasionally impossible to avoid remarking on the same features that they do; and in a reader of this scope it has been impossible to engage in discussion with these commentaries or give them explicit credit for every specific debt I owe them. Scholars familiar with their work will realize the level of my indebtedness; and I am grateful to all the authors whose work I have used. Any errors or idiosyncracies in interpretation are my own.

I am grateful to Jane Chaplin for reading over the Introduction, and to Josh Hainy and Larissa Carlson for their work compiling the Vocabulary. A dedicated group of Latin students read these passages with me, asked useful questions, and made valuable suggestions: I want to thank Brie Bridegum, Desiree Brown, Larissa Carlson, Desiree Gerner, Josh Hainy, Aaron Heinrich, Rachel Reynolds, Natalie Simons, Susan Stater and Chris Todd. The anonymous readers for the press have saved me from myself again and again, and I owe them a tremendous debt of gratitude. Ronnie Ancona has been a tactful and patient editor for the series; and I am grateful to her, as I am to the equally patient and helpful Laurie Haight Keenan, editor for the press.

Many years ago Marleen B. Flory introduced me to Livy; I would like to dedicate this volume to her memory.

Mary Jaeger
Eugene, Oregon

Introduction

⤳ *Livy's life and times*

Of the three great historians of Rome, Livy tells us the least about himself. Unlike Sallust before and Tacitus after him, Livy says nothing directly about his origins or background, with the result that what little we know of his life comes from external, and not always trustworthy, sources. The late antique scholar Jerome gives Livy's dates as 59 BCE to 17 CE. These dates may be five years off, and Livy may have lived 64 BCE to 12 CE. Other external sources tell us that he was from Patavium (modern Padua) in the Po delta, a large and prosperous town in Cisalpine Gaul. (An epitaph commemorating a T. Livius who had a wife and two sons attests to the family presence in the area.) Although subject to Rome by 174 BCE, Patavium enjoyed local autonomy, as well as a reputation for strict moral conservatism. Livy expresses his local patriotism implicitly by writing of Antenor's settlement of the area near Patavium (Book 1.1.1–3) before mentioning Aeneas' arrival in Latium.

Whether or not Jerome's dates are correct, Livy was almost contemporary with Augustus (63 BCE–14 CE). Thus he was an impressionable youth during the years of conflict between Caesar and Pompey (48–46 BCE) and a young man during the long period of civil war (44–31 BCE) that followed Caesar's assassination. He was, therefore, a witness to both the destruction of the civil war and the restoration that followed under Caesar's heir Augustus. Internal evidence combined with Jerome's dates suggests that Livy began to write between 35 and 30 BCE. The political conflict and violence that occurred during his youth would have influenced profoundly the thoughts of this intelligent and creative observer as he conceived and mapped out his project.

Livy's origins and background, then, explain to some degree his interest in ethics and moral lessons, his pro-Republican attitude, and the virtues with which he invests Rome's early leaders. There is some evidence—evidence that, however, lends itself to different interpretations—that Livy knew and was on good terms with Augustus. The Augustan regime's endorsement of such Roman values as *pietas*, *virtus*, and *iustitia*, if not its creeping monarchism, probably appealed to Livy. The overall impression is of a thinker who is independent in his judgement of people and events, yet sympathetic to the Augustan program for restoring Rome physically and morally.

Livy had the education expected of a talented and well-off young man of his place and time. Such an education included early study of Greek and Latin literature, followed by a thorough grounding in rhetoric, which generally included practice in the art of declamation. This art involved the crafting and presentation of both fictive speeches on legal matters, a form of composition known as *controversia*, and fictive speeches, known as *suasoriae*, that deliberated on historical or mythological subjects. Livy's early study of poets and historians influenced the way in which he imagined the past. His skill at imagining the psychology of historical figures as they encountered various dilemmas, and at presenting events in a lively and convincing manner, could stem from the practice of declamation.

Although, according to Seneca, Livy wrote some philosophical dialogues in his youth, he appears to have devoted his adult life solely to writing history; and he seems to have written history at the expense of any other significant activity. This is a conclusion drawn from the size and scope of his historical project and from some negative facts: first, there is no evidence that Livy ever held political office nor that he had any military experience. (Although that is just what it is: no evidence.) Nor is there evidence that Livy traveled widely. He was familiar with the Po valley. His references to Rome's topography suggest that he spent some time in the city, the place that offered him the most access to the works of earlier historians, especially the Latin ones; but, aside from saying that he saw the estate of Scipio Africanus at Liternum, a town near Cumae, Livy does not write of his own travels.

This absence of evidence for a life involved in politics and military affairs has at times led scholars to judge Livy's history more for what it is *not* than for what it is, and more for what it lacks than for what it has. For example, we find in Livy's history neither the emphasis on eyewitness information so pronounced in the great Athenian historian, Thucydides, nor the interest in geographical autopsy and political analysis so characteristic of the Hellenistic historian of Rome, Polybius. Both of these men took part in politics, and could speak of war from personal experience. Yet, because the books of Livy's history that covered contemporary events are lost, we cannot fault him too much for not consulting eyewitnesses; and, although Livy preferred the dramatic presentation of politics in action to Polybian analysis, his history, as we shall see, shows that he had thought carefully about the impact of past events on his contemporary world, about the uses of the recorded past, and about ways in which to represent it.

☙ Livy's work, subject and scope

The traditional title of Livy's work is *Ab Urbe Condita Libri* "Books From the Founding of the City" (= *AUC*). To set about writing a detailed narrative history centered on Rome, one that covered events from the city's origins into the Augustan Age, was to undertake a massive and ambitious task. We do not know what Livy envisioned as his entire project nor if he completed the work he had planned. We know that he wrote at least 142 books, because, although only thirty-five books have survived, there are multiple summaries of his work from the third and fourth centuries CE. The most extensive of these covers 142 books (with those for Books 136 and 137 inexplicably missing). The 142 books begin with the immediate aftermath of the fall of Troy (*iam primum omnium satis constat Troia capta in ceteros saeuitum esse Troianos* . . . "it is first of all agreed that, after Troy was taken, the rest of the Trojans suffered the fierce consequences . . ."); their last dateable event is the death of Tiberius' brother Drusus in 9 BCE. The surviving books are 1–10 and 21–45. Books 1–10 cover the period from the founding of the city to Rome's conquest of the Italian peninsula; the lost Books 11–21 cover events to the end of the

First Punic War; Books 21–30, the Second Punic War; Books 31–45, the Second and Third Macedonian Wars. A few fragments of the lost books survive, such as, for example, a passage from Book 120 quoted by Seneca, which preserves Livy's description of the murder of Cicero in 43 BCE. Books 121 and following may have been published after Augustus' death.

Massive as it is, Livy's project does not lack structure. The first part of the work shows a pattern of arrangement by groups of five books (pentads) and groups of ten (decades). Books 1–5 take the reader from the founding of the city to its near-destruction by invading Gauls; Book 6 begins with a new preface and the rebuilding of the city; and Books 6–10 cover Rome's conquest of the Italian peninsula. Books 21–30, one of the most satisfying parts of the history to read as a unit, recount the war against Hannibal, with Carthage ascendant in most of 21–25 and Rome turning the tables in most of 26–30. Books 31–45 relate the second and third Macedonian wars. In his use of books and groups of books to give structure to a larger work, Livy shares an interest with other writers of the Augustan era, who likewise took pains both in constructing individual books and in arranging multi-book works. The first three books of Horace's *Odes*, for example, show a careful arrangement of the poems within each book as well as a strong sense of opening and closure at the beginning and end of the entire collection. Likewise the twelve books of Vergil's *Aeneid* include both an Odyssean half, Aeneas' journey to Italy in Books 1–6, and an Iliadic one, Aeneas' battle for a foothold in Italy in Books 7–12.

The result of Livy's labors was bulky and expensive. The first century CE poet Martial already knew of an abridged version: his book of mottoes for party favors includes one for a summary of Livy (14.190): *pellibus exiguis artatur Livius ingens / quem mea non totum bibliotheca capit* ("within meager parchments is compressed huge Livy, whom my entire library does not hold").

∽ *Livy's sources*

Modern historians use primary sources, such as public records, private papers, transcripts of speeches, and interviews with eyewitnesses. To some degree ancient historians writing contemporary history—Thucydides, for example—did this as well. But ancient historians writing non-contemporary history mostly relied on the accounts of other historians. This does not make for good historiography by modern standards; and even the Hellenistic historian Polybius (c. 200–c.188 BCE) said that anyone who wanted to write political history needed to examine documents, visit sites, and take part in political life. But in general the standards of the ancients were not ours. Historiography was a creative art: writers of history started with what modern scholars would recognize as documented fact, or at least as attested tradition, and represented the events surrounding it in a compelling and persuasive manner, even if doing so meant departing from their sources. Moreover, ancient historians tended to represent their relationships with their sources in terms of emulation and competition. The result is that ancient historiography is by nature intertextual, with historians using previous narratives both as sources of information and as backgrounds against which to distinguish themselves within the tradition. In his preface, Livy refers to the "crowd of writers," *turba scriptorum*, in which he feels he might be lost; and he consistently positions and repositions the *AUC* relative to the works of his literary rivals. His work comments on and contributes to the literary tradition, even as it preserves the memory of Rome's past.

Livy's sources vary according to his subject. Oral traditions, including historical drama, stories about monuments and place-names, as well as family traditions, all grafted onto a mythical rootstock, formed the largely legendary account of Rome in the regal period. In addition, surveys of early Rome appeared in the work of the city's first historian, Fabius Pictor, and in the *Annales* of the early Roman epic poet, Ennius (239–169 BCE). For the period of the republic, Livy primarily used the works of earlier Roman "annalistic" historians, who produced accounts of Rome's past structured by the consular year. These annalists may have worked from priestly records, known as the *annales maximi*, which contained such information as the names of magistrates, prodigies, the dedication of temples, and possibly military achievements or setbacks. The annalistic form of narrative followed a stylized pattern, beginning the year with the election of magistrates and the listing of religious portents, and then moving on to cover events at home and abroad. For the first decade Livy used the works of the late Roman annalists, Valerius Antias, Claudius Quadrigarius, and Licinius Macer, all from the early first century BCE, as well as that of Aelius Tubero, who survived into the Augustan period. For the third decade, Livy could use Fabius Pictor's Greek monograph on the Second Punic War, as well as the Latin history of Coelius Antipater, who used both Roman sources and a pro-Carthaginian account. Livy also used the Hellenistic historian, Polybius, who wrote in Greek, as a source for the Second Punic War, although where he began using him directly and not through an intermediary author is still debated. For the period covered by Books 31–45, however, Livy's major source was clearly Polybius, whose work he adapted and adjusted to suit his purposes. For information about events in Rome, Livy continued to use the Roman annalists, especially Valerius Antias and Claudius Quadrigarius.

Livy probably kept a scroll of his primary source for a given episode unrolled before him as he wrote, so that he could follow it, sometimes in detail, and make corrections, comments on variants, and alterations and improvements in sentence structure. (He even comments on the ruder taste of his literary predecessors, in the story of Manlius and the Gaul from Book 7, which is included in this volume. It is one of the rare passages for which we also have the version of an annalist, Claudius Quadrigarius, as well. Comparing the two is a good way of seeing how Livy shapes the received tradition.) Livy had also read other earlier Roman writers, including Sallust, Cicero, and Caesar, who influenced his prose style and were probably sources for events in the later, lost, books. Important, but distinct from sources for information about past events, were the

writers, such as the great Greek historians Herodotus and Thucydides, who shaped Livy's patterns of thought and thus contributed
to shaping his narrative.

∾ *Ideas*

Preserving the memory of the past was an avowed purpose for historians from Herodotus on. Although Livy said that his subject was
the achievements (*res gestae*) of the Roman people, he made it clear
that his own work was an achievement too, a *res* accomplished on
Rome's behalf in the form of a *monumentum*, a reminder, one that
commemorated the past by engaging the attention of the present
and engaging it for a purpose. According to Livy, Rome was in crisis. Luxury, greed, and personal ambition had destroyed the moral
character that had once made Rome great and won it an empire. He
described the city metaphorically as being in such a condition that
it could endure neither the illness it suffered nor the remedy for it.
The task Livy set himself was to identify and celebrate early Rome's
strict moral character, elements of which he found in individual men
and women, and in groups. He also aimed to trace the process by
which luxury, greed, and personal ambition entered Rome, attacked
such fine qualities as courage, nobility, and self-sacrifice, and un-
dermined that early Roman character. The recorded past was useful
both for understanding this process of rise and decline and for re-
sisting, as much as possible, the final collapse, because history provided contemporary Rome with moral examples, both good and bad,
to follow or avoid.

Livy was interested in the lessons offered by the record of the
wide variety of human experience. Thus, in the small sample of his
work contained in this volume, we see the founder of the city mur-
dering his brother; three figures, an obscure soldier, a young woman, and a young aristocrat, separately defying the invading enemy;
the scion of an accomplished family engaging an enemy soldier in
single combat; Rome's most terrifying enemy displaying extraordinary qualities as a leader; a Roman general trying to put heart into
his inexperienced army; an awful model of Roman determination

found among the carnage of the battlefield; and a female ex-slave being comforted by the mother-in-law of a consul. Moreover, although the stories of the obscure soldier, young woman, and young aristocrat, that is, those of Horatius at the bridge, Mucius Scaevola, and Cloelia, can be read each alone as an example of heroic behavior, the three together create a composite picture of Roman moral character that embraces the socially obscure as well as the aristocrat, the female as well as the male. Likewise the exposure of the cult of Bacchus begins with the female ex-slave (and prostitute), Hispala, demonstrating morally exemplary behavior; it ends with the Roman elite, the consuls and Senate, restoring social order. In Livy examples of good and bad behavior can come from anywhere, although most come from the aristocracy.

These stories also show how Livy preferred demonstration to theoretical discussion: the reaction of consuls and senate to the cult of Bacchus exemplifies the actions of an efficient if repressive government; and Hannibal's staging of single combat between Gauls and Carthaginians both makes very clear to his army its precarious situation and displays Hannibal's own brilliance as a leader.

This focus on human behavior in all its variety largely determines Livy's treatment of religion. In spite of numerous references to omens, portents, and the dedication of temples, and in spite of many of his characters' references to the gods, Livy approaches religion from the human side. His narrative shows Roman *pietas* and lapses in *pietas* influencing events rather than the gods acting in order to influence events. When, for example, early in the Second Punic War, the consul-elect Flaminius sneaks away from the city without having fulfilled his ritual observations, disaster follows in the form of the Roman defeat at Lake Trasimene. The Romans act with increasing responsibility towards the gods starting from the aftermath of Cannae, and success in war attends these efforts. This focus on human behavior and this human perspective on events as opposed to the divine are features that distinguish ancient historiography from epic. A comparison of any book of the *Aeneid* and any book of Livy quickly makes this clear.

∾ *Livy's artistry*

Readers encountering Livy for the first time will immediately appreciate his talents as a storyteller, one who conveys clearly and with effective detail his accounts of individuals acting for Rome's good or harm and who accents their deeds with memorable words. Indeed, Livy's artistry appears in many facets of his work from the large scale to the small: the arrangement of the history into pentads and decades; the cyclical marking of the passage of time through the annalistic framework; the organization of events into unified episodes that have their own beginnings, middles and ends; and the lively mixture of narrative with direct and indirect speech.

This last feature came to ancient historiography from epic poetry through Herodotus, who included both dialogue and speeches in his history of the Persian Wars. Set speeches at crucial moments became a standard element of historical writing, especially for writers following the precedent set by Thucydides, who includes, for example, Pericles' famous funeral oration at the end of the first year's fighting, and the speeches of Nicias and Alcibiades debating about the Athenian expedition against Sicily. Like other ancient historians, Livy does not try, or claim, to replicate the very words used by his speakers; rather, he gives them words that portray their characters and the nature of the situations in which they find themselves. Thus the paired speeches delivered by the elder Scipio and Hannibal before the Romans and Carthaginians meet in battle for the first time tell us about the personalities and mental qualities of the speakers. Scipio's speech displays his concern for his men together with an arrogance born of ignorance. (He does not yet know he is up against one of the greatest generals of all time.) Hannibal's makes clear his determination and his ability to inspire his followers. Moreover, these speeches from the first book on the war (Book 21) are balanced by another pair from the last (Book 30), only the latter pair are delivered by Hannibal and by Scipio's son (the future Africanus), when the two meet before the decisive Roman victory at Zama.

Livy wrote in Latin that the rhetorician Quintilian characterized as being of "milky richness" (*lactea ubertas*). It seems to have been a reaction against the compressed and contorted Thucydidean style of Sallust. Yet milk is not clear water, and Livy, aiming for neither Caesar's stark simplicity nor Cicero's balanced periods, adds richness to his prose in several ways. One of them is by writing in a variety of styles. I compare here only two of these, the highly paratactic and the highly periodic. First, because he uses the annalistic framework, Livy often begins a year's narrative with a list, which generally includes the inauguration of magistrates, the assignment of provinces, the appearance of portents, the performance of games, and the dedication of temples. Such passages may seem monotonous to modern readers, but they appealed to the antiquarian interests of Augustan Romans and marked the passage of time with dignity and even ritual solemnity. Here is one from the beginning of 204 BCE (29.11.9–14). I have not translated it here, because the structure of the Latin sentences is the important point:

> *Q. Caecilius Metellus dictator ab consule in Bruttiis comitiorum causa dictus exercitusque eius dimissus, magister equitum L. Veturius Philo. Comitia per dictatorem habita. Consules facti M. Cornelius Cethegus P. Sempronius Tuditanus absens cum prouinciam Graeciam haberet. Praetores inde creati Ti. Claudius Nero M. Maricius Ralla L. Scribonius Libo M. Pomponius Matho. Comitiis peractis dictator sese magistratu abdicauit. Ludi Romani ter, plebeii septiens instaurati. Curules erant aediles Cn. et L. Cornelii Lentuli. Lucius Hispaniam prouinciam habebat; absens creatus absens eum honorem gessit. Ti. Claudius Asellus et M. Iunius Pennus plebeii aediles fuerunt. Aedem Virtutis eo anno ad portam Capenam M. Marcellus dedicauit septimo decimo anno postquam a patre eius primo consulatu uota in Gallia ad Clastidium fuerat. Et flamen Martialis eo anno est mortuus M. Aemilius Regillus.*

The selection of a dictator for the purpose of holding elections; his master of horse; the election of magistrates, and the names of the elected; which games were put on and under which aediles; the dedication of a temple, and the death of a priest—Livy conveys this information in short sentences in which there is almost no subordination of one clause to another. This passage, in fact, which contains fourteen personal names and six place names, has only one ablative absolute (*comitiis peractis*) and two subordinate clauses (*cum . . . haberet*; *postquam . . . uota . . . fuerat*).

In contrast, Livy's periodic sentences offer us our earliest examples of a fully developed periodic structure in historiography. Livy modeled his style on that of Cicero and Caesar, but avoided Caesar's tendency to repeat constructions for the sake of clarity and used fewer parallel constructions in his sentence structure than did Cicero. In addition, Livy's periodic sentences make extensive use of participles to convey a great amount of information in a relatively small space. Consider, for example, Livy's description of Hannibal's swearing that he will be an enemy to Rome:

> *Fama est etiam Hannibalem, annorum ferme nouem,*
> *pueriliter blandientem patri Hamilcari ut duceretur*
> *in Hispaniam, cum perfecto Africo bello exercitum*
> *eo traiecturus sacrificaret, altaribus admotum tactis*
> *sacris iure iurando adactum, se cum primum posset*
> *hostem fore populo Romano.*

Although this sentence is less than a third the length of the annalistic passage quoted above, it has many more subordinate elements. After the introductory *fama est*, readers encounter the following: the subject of the indirect statement, Hannibal; his age in apposition; a present active participle modifying him and introducing a subordinate clause; a circumstantial *cum*-clause, which includes an ablative absolute in the perfect describing what Hamilcar has done, and a future participle modifying him by describing what he is about to do; another participle modifying Hannibal; an ablative absolute relating his actions; and finally, yet another participial phrase modifying Hannibal and introducing the substance of his oath, which is an indirect statement including yet another *cum*-clause. The result is a complex sentence, which changes constructions too quickly to become tedious.

Other features of Livy's prose include the use of archaisms and poeticisms, which tend to appear in the books covering the legendary period or elsewhere when Livy discusses the distant past, and the deployment of such rhetorical figures as asyndeton (omission of conjunctions); alliteration (e.g., *Romulum Remumque cupido cepit*); chiastic word order (ABBA); and such forms of amplification as *congeries verborum* (an accumulation of words; e.g., crossing the Alps, the Carthaginians are *contusi ac debilitati inter saxa rupesque*, "broken and bruised among the rocks and cliffs"). The commentary points out specific instances of these.

∾ Reception

Livy's history was famous from the start. Pliny (*Ep.*2.3.8) tells the story of a man from Gades (Cadiz), who came all the way to Rome just to look upon Livy. Quintilian says that he prefers Livy to Sallust for the novice reader. The biographer Suetonius mentions Livy three times in his *Lives* of the Caesars: Gaius (Caligula) wanted to banish Livy's works and portrait busts from the libraries because he found him wordy and inaccurate (Livy was in good company, because Gaius wanted to do the same to Vergil and to suppress the poems of Homer as well); Livy encouraged the young Claudius in the writing of history; and the emperor Domitian had one Mettius Pompusienus executed for, among other offenses, carrying about a collection of speeches of kings and generals excerpted from Livy. Tacitus pays Livy homage by alluding to his preface in the opening lines of his *Annales* and at times imitating him. For example, he models the character of Livia, to some degree, on that of the ambitious and aggressive Etruscan wives in Livy, Book 1. The epic poet Silius Italicus used Livy as a source for his *Bellum Punicum*. In addition, the second-century historian Florus, the late fourth-century historian Eutropius, and the late fourth- to early fifth-century Julius Obsequens, who catalogued prodigies, all used Livy as a major source.

The fourteenth-century humanist, Petrarch, was the first person since antiquity to have a text of Livy substantially as complete as the one we have today. He writes of his frustration at searching for but never finding the manuscript of the lost second decade. Petrarch used Livy for the Roman material in two of his prose works, the *Libri Rerum Memorandarum* and the *De Viris Illustribus*. In addition, his epic, *Africa*, which takes as its subject Scipio Africanus' victory over Carthage, draws on the final books of Livy's account of the Second Punic War. The political philosopher Niccolo Machiavelli (1469–1527) drew on his careful reading of Livy for his study of Republicanism (*Discourses on the First Ten Books of Titus Livius*, 1513–1517). The nineteenth-century British politician, historian, essayist, and poet, Lord Macaulay, wrote a series of poems titled *Lays of Ancient Rome*, which were inspired by an ancient reference to the singing of sagas at early Roman banquets. The most famous of the *Lays* was an account of Horatius at the Bridge, based on stories from Book 2. Memorized and recited by schoolchildren until memorizing fell out of fashion, it is still a stirring read today.

∾ Suggested reading
Introductory
Dorey, T. A., ed. *Latin Historians*. New York, 1966.

Kraus, C. S., and A. J. Woodman. *Latin Historians. Greece & Rome. New Surveys in the Classics* No. 27. Oxford, 1997.

Ogilvie, R. M. "Livy." In the *Cambridge History of Classical Literature*, Vol. 2: *Latin Literature*. Edited by E. J. Kenney and W. V. Clausen. Cambridge, 1982, 162–70.

Commentaries, dictionaries, and grammaers
Bennett, C. *New Latin Grammar*. Wauconda, IL, 2006.

Briscoe, J. *A Commentary on Livy Books 38–40*. Oxford, 2008.

Glare, P. G. W., ed. *Oxford Latin Dictionary*. Oxford, 1982. (= OLD)

Greenough, J. B. *Livy, Books I and II*. New Rochelle, NY, 1976.

———. *Livy, Books XXI and XXII*. Boston and London, 1896.

Forsyth, G. *Livy, Book XXXIX*. Bryn Mawr, PA, 1994.

Kraus, C. S. *Livy, Ab Urbe Condita VI*. Cambridge, 1994.

Oakley S. P. *A Commentary on Livy Books VI–X*, Volume II. Oxford, 1998.

Ogilvie, R. M. *A Commentary on Livy Books I–V*. 2nd ed. Oxford, 1970.

Richardson, L. jr. *A New Topographical Dictionary of Ancient Rome*. Baltimore and London, 1992.

The history as a whole

Chaplin, J. D. *Livy's Exemplary History*. New York, 2000.

Chaplin, J. D., and C. S. Kraus, eds. *Oxford Readings in Classical Studies: Livy*. New York, 2009.

Feldherr, A. *Spectacle and Society in Livy's History*. Berkeley and Los Angeles, 1998.

Forsyth, G. *Livy and Early Rome, A Study in Historical Method and Judgment. Historia Einzelschriften* 132. Stuttgart, 1999.

Jaeger, M. *Livy's Written Rome*. Ann Arbor, 1997.

Luce, T. J. *Livy: The Composition of His History*. Princeton, 1977.

Walsh, P. G. *Livy: His Historical Aims and Methods*. Cambridge, 1961.

Particular aspects of the history

Briscoe, J. "The First Decade." In *Livy*. Edited by T. A. Dorey. London, 1971.

Burck, E. "The Third Decade." In *Livy*. Edited by T. A. Dorey. London, 1971.

Levene, D. S. *Religion in Livy*. Leiden, 1993.

———. *Livy on the Hannibalic War*. Oxford and New York, 2010.

Miles, G. *Livy: Reconstructing Early Rome*. Ithaca and London, 1995.

Pagán, V. E. *Conspiracy Narratives in Roman History*. Austin, 2004.

Roller, M. "Exemplarity in Roman Culture: the Cases of Horatius Cocles and Cloelia." *Classical Philology* 99.1 (2004) 1–56.

Scafuro, A. "Livy's Comic Narrative of the Bacchanalia." *Helios* 16 (1989) 119–42.

Walsh, P. G. "Making a Drama out of a Crisis: Livy on the Bacchanalia." *Greece & Rome* ser. 2, vol. 43 (1996) 188–203.

The rediscovery of Livy

Billanovich, G. "Petrarch and the Textual Tradition of Livy." *Journal of the Warburg and Courtauld Institutes* 14 (1951) 137–208.

Latin Text

- I have retained intervocalic *u* instead of *v* throughout.
- Selections from books 1–5 are from R. M. Ogilvie, *Titi Livi Ab Vrbe Condita, Tomus I, Libri I–V*, Oxford, 1974.
- The Selection from Book 7 is from C. F. Walters and R. S. Conway, *Titi Livi Ab Vrbe Condita, Tomus II, Libri VI–X*, Oxford, 1914.
- Selections from Books 21–22, are from C. F. Walters and R. S. Conway, *Titi Livi Ab Vrbe Condita, Tomus III, Libri XXI–XXV*, Oxford, 1929.
    - I diverge from the Oxford text at 21.44.2, where I follow T. A. Dorey's 1971 Teubner edition in printing *<pro> patria instead of <ob> patriam*, and at 21.44.7, where I follow the Teubner edition in printing the conjecture of H. J. Mueller (*Et inde si decessero*).
    - The Oxford text prints: *Adimis etiam Hispanias et, si inde, cessero, in Africam transcendes. <Transcendes> autem? Transcendisse dico.*
    - The text printed in this volume is: *Adimis etiam Hispanias, et, inde <si de>cessero, in Africam transcendes. <transcendes> autem? transcendisse dico.*
- Excerpts from Book 39 are from P. G. Walsh, *Titi Livi Ab Vrbe Condita*, Tomus VI, Libri XXXVI–XL, Oxford 1999.

∾ *From Livy's preface*
Praef. 6–10

Quae ante conditam condendamue urbem poeticis magis **6**
decora fabulis quam incorruptis rerum gestarum monu-
mentis traduntur, ea nec adfirmare nec refellere in animo
est. Datur haec uenia antiquitati ut miscendo humana **7**
5 diuinis primordia urbium augustiora faciat; et si cui
populo licere oportet consecrare origines suas et ad deos
referre auctores, ea belli gloria est populo Romano ut cum
suum conditorisque sui parentem Martem potissimum ferat,
tam et hoc gentes humanae patiantur aequo animo quam
10 imperium patiuntur. Sed haec et his similia utcumque **8**
animaduersa aut existimata erunt haud in magno equidem
ponam discrimine: ad illa mihi pro se quisque acriter **9**
intendat animum, quae uita, qui mores fuerint, per quos
uiros quibusque artibus domi militiaeque et partum et
15 auctum imperium sit; labante deinde paulatim disciplina
uelut dissidentes primo mores sequatur animo, deinde ut
magis magisque lapsi sint, tum ire coeperint praecipites,
donec ad haec tempora quibus nec uitia nostra nec remedia
pati possumus peruentum est. Hoc illud est praecipue in **10**
20 cognitione rerum salubre ac frugiferum, omnis te exempli
documenta in inlustri posita monumento intueri; inde tibi
tuaeque rei publicae quod imitere capias, inde foedum
inceptu foedum exitu quod uites.

✑ *From the first decade* (*Books 1–10*)
The founding of Rome, 1.6.3–7.3

Ita Numitori Albana re permissa Romulum Remumque   **6.**3
cupido cepit in iis locis, ubi expositi ubique educati erant
urbis condendae. Et supererat multitudo Albanorum Lati-
norumque; ad id pastores quoque accesserant, qui omnes
5 facile spem facerent, paruam Albam, paruum Lauinium
prae ea urbe quae conderetur fore. Interuenit deinde his   4
cogitationibus auitum malum, regni cupido, atque inde
foedum certamen coortum a satis miti principio. Quoniam
gemini essent nec aetatis uerecundia discrimen facere
10 posset, ut di quorum tutelae ea loca essent auguriis legerent
qui nomen nouae urbi daret, qui conditam imperio regeret,
Palatium Romulus, Remus Auentinum ad inaugurandum
templa capiunt.

Priori Remo augurium uenisse fertur, sex uoltures; iam-   7
15 que nuntiato augurio cum duplex numerus Romulo se
ostendisset, utrumque regem sua multitudo consalutaue-
rat: tempore illi praecepto, at hi numero auium regnum   2
trahebant. Inde cum altercatione congressi certamine
irarum ad caedem uertuntur; ibi in turba ictus Remus
20 cecidit. Volgatior fama est ludibrio fratris Remum nouos
transiluisse muros; inde ab irato Romulo, cum uerbis
quoque increpitans adiecisset, 'Sic deinde, quicumque alius
transiliet moenia mea', interfectum. Ita solus potitus im-   3
perio Romulus; condita urbs conditoris nomine appellata.

Horatius at the bridge, 2.10.1–13

Cum hostes adessent, pro se quisque in urbem ex agris   **10**

demigrant; urbem ipsam saepiunt praesidiis. Alia muris,

alia Tiberi obiecto uidebantur tuta: pons sublicius iter   2

paene hostibus dedit, ni unus uir fuisset, Horatius Cocles;

5   id munimentum illo die fortuna urbis Romanae habuit.

Qui positus forte in statione pontis cum captum repentino   3

impetu Ianiculum atque inde citatos decurrere hostes uidis-

set trepidamque turbam suorum arma ordinesque relin-

quere, reprehensans singulos, obsistens obtestansque deum

10   et hominum fidem testabatur nequiquam deserto praesidio

eos fugere; si transitum pontem a tergo reliquissent, iam   4

plus hostium in Palatio Capitolioque quam in Ianiculo fore.

Itaque monere, praedicere ut pontem ferro, igni, quacum-

que ui possint, interrumpant: se impetum hostium, quan-

15   tum corpore uno posset obsisti, excepturum. Vadit inde in   5

primum aditum pontis, insignisque inter conspecta ceden-

tium pugnae terga obuersis comminus ad ineundum

proelium armis, ipso miraculo audaciae obstupefecit hostes.

Duos tamen cum eo pudor tenuit, Sp. Larcium ac T.   6

20   Herminium, ambos claros genere factisque. Cum his   7

primam periculi procellam et quod tumultuosissimum

pugnae erat parumper sustinuit; deinde eos quoque ipsos

exigua parte pontis relicta reuocantibus qui rescindebant

cedere in tutum coegit. Circumferens inde truces minaciter   8

25   oculos ad proceres Etruscorum nunc singulos prouocare,

nunc increpare omnes: seruitia regum superborum, suae

libertatis immemores alienam oppugnatum uenire. Cunctati   9

main verb

aliquamdiu sunt, (dum alius alium, ut proelium incipiant,
circumspectant) pudor deinde commouit aciem, et clamore
30 sublato undique in unum hostem tela coniciunt. Quae (cum   10
in obiecto cuncta scuto haesissent, neque ille minus obsti-
natus ingenti pontem obtineret gradu) iam impetu cona-
bantur detrudere uirum, (cum simul fragor rupti pontis,
simul clamor Romanorum, alacritate perfecti operis sub-
35 latus, pauore subito impetum sustinuit.) Tum Cocles ('Tibe-   11
rine pater,' inquit, 'te sancte precor, haec arma et hunc   *indirect command*
~atulis   militem propitio flumine accipias.') Ita sic armatus in Tiberim desiluit multisque superincidentibus telis incolumis
ad suos tranauit, rem ausus plus famae habituram ad
40 posteros quam fidei. Grata erga tantam uirtutem ciuitas   12
fuit; statua in comitio posita; agri quantum uno die circum-
arauit, datum. Priuata quoque inter publicos honores   13
studia eminebant; nam in magna inopia pro domesticis
copiis unusquisque ei aliquid, fraudans se ipse uictu suo,
45 contulit.

Mucius Scaevola, 2.12.1–16

Obsidio erat nihilo minus et frumenti cum summa cari-   **12**
tate inopia, sedendoque expugnaturum se urbem spem
Porsenna habebat, cum C. Mucius, adulescens nobilis, cui   2
indignum uidebatur populum Romanum seruientem cum
5 sub regibus esset nullo bello nec ab hostibus ullis obsessum
esse, liberum eundem populum ab iisdem Etruscis obsideri
quorum saepe exercitus fuderit—itaque magno audacique   3
aliquo facinore eam indignitatem uindicandam ratus, primo

sua sponte penetrare in hostium castra constituit; dein   4
10 metuens ne si consulum iniussu et ignaris omnibus iret, forte
deprehensus a custodibus Romanis retraheretur ut transfuga, fortuna tum urbis crimen adfirmante, senatum adit.
'Transire Tiberim,' inquit, 'patres, et intrare, si possim,   5
castra hostium uolo, non praedo nec populationum in
15 uicem ultor; maius si di iuuant in animo est facinus.'
Adprobant patres; abdito intra uestem ferro proficiscitur.
Vbi eo uenit, in confertissima turba prope regium tribu-   6
nal constitit. Ibi cum stipendium militibus forte daretur et   7
scriba cum rege sedens pari fere ornatu multa ageret eum-
20 <que> milites uolgo adirent, timens sciscitari uter Porsenna
esset, ne ignorando regem semet ipse aperiret quis esset, quo
temere traxit fortuna facinus, scribam pro rege obtruncat.
Vadentem inde qua per trepidam turbam cruento mucrone   8
sibi ipse fecerat uiam, cum concursu ad clamorem facto
25 comprehensum regii satellites retraxissent, ante tribunal
regis destitutus, tum quoque inter tantas fortunae minas
metuendus magis quam metuens, 'Romanus sum' inquit,   9
'ciuis; C. Mucium uocant. Hostis hostem occidere uolui,
nec ad mortem minus animi est quam fuit ad caedem; et
30 facere et pati fortia Romanum est. Nec unus in te ego hos   10
animos gessi; longus post me ordo est idem petentium decus.
Proinde in hoc discrimen, si iuuat, accingere, ut in singulas
horas capite dimices tuo, ferrum hostemque in uestibulo
habeas regiae. Hoc tibi iuuentus Romana indicimus bellum.
35 Nullam aciem, nullum proelium timueris; uni tibi et cum   11
singulis res erit.' Cum rex simul ira incensus periculoque   12

conterritus circumdari ignes minitabundus iuberet nisi
expromeret propere quas insidiarum sibi minas per ambages
iaceret, 'En tibi,' inquit, 'ut sentias quam uile corpus sit iis   13
40 qui magnam gloriam uident'; dextramque accenso ad sacrificium foculo inicit. Quam cum uelut alienato ab sensu torreret animo, prope attonitus miraculo rex cum ab sede sua
prosiluisset amouerique ab altaribus iuuenem iussisset, 'Tu   14
uero abi', inquit, 'in te magis quam in me hostilia ausus.
45 Iuberem macte uirtute esse, si pro mea patria ista uirtus
staret; nunc iure belli liberum te, intactum inuiolatumque
hinc dimitto.' Tunc Mucius, quasi remunerans meritum,   15
'Quando quidem' inquit 'est apud te uirtuti honos, ut beneficio tuleris a me quod minis nequisti, trecenti coniurauimus
50 principes iuuentutis Romanae ut in te hac uia grassaremur.
Mea prima sors fuit; ceteri ut cuiusque ceciderit primi   16
quoad te opportunum fortuna dederit, suo quisque tempore
aderunt.'

Cloelia, 2.13.6–11

Ergo ita honorata uirtute,   **13.**6
feminae quoque ad publica decora excitatae, et Cloelia
uirgo una ex obsidibus, cum castra Etruscorum forte haud
procul ripa Tiberis locata essent, frustrata custodes, dux
5 agminis uirginum inter tela hostium Tiberim tranauit,
sospitesque omnes Romam ad propinquos restituit. Quod   7
ubi regi nuntiatum est, primo incensus ira oratores Romam
misit ad Cloeliam obsidem deposcendam: alias haud magni
facere. Deinde in admirationem uersus, supra Coclites   8

10 Muciosque dicere id facinus esse, et prae se ferre quemadmodum si non dedatur obses, pro rupto foedus se hab-
   turum, sic deditam <intactam> inuiolatamque ad suos
   remissurum. Vtrimque constitit fides; et Romani pignus   9
   pacis ex foedere restituerunt, et apud regem Etruscum non
15 tuta solum sed honorata etiam uirtus fuit, laudatamque
   uirginem parte obsidum se donare dixit; ipsa quos uellet
   legeret. Productis omnibus elegisse impubes dicitur; quod   10
   et uirginitati decorum et consensu obsidum ipsorum
   probabile erat eam aetatem potissimum liberari ab hoste
20 quae maxime opportuna iniuriae esset. Pace redintegrata   11
   Romani nouam in femina uirtutem nouo genere honoris,
   statua equestri, donauere; in summa Sacra uia fuit posita
   uirgo insidens equo.

Manlius and the Gaul, 7.9.6–10.14

   Dictator cum tumultus Gallici causa iustitium edixisset,   **9.**6
   omnes iuniores sacramento adegit ingentique exercitu ab
   urbe profectus in citeriore ripa Anienis castra posuit. Pons   7
   in medio erat, neutris rumpentibus ne timoris indicium
5 esset. Proelia de occupando ponte crebra erant, nec qui
   poterentur incertis uiribus satis discerni poterat. Tum   8
   eximia corporis magnitudine in uacuum pontem Gallus pro-
   cessit et quantum maxima uoce potuit 'quem nunc' inquit
   'Roma uirum fortissimum habet, procedat agedum ad pug-
10 nam, ut noster duorum euentus ostendat utra gens bello sit
   melior.' Diu inter primores iuuenum Romanorum silentium   **10**
   fuit, cum et abnuere certamen uererentur et praecipuam

sortem periculi petere nollent; tum T. Manlius L. filius,   2
qui patrem a uexatione tribunicia uindicauerat, ex statione
15 ad dictatorem pergit; 'iniussu tuo' inquit, 'imperator, extra
ordinem nunquam pugnauerim, non si certam uictoriam ui-
deam: si tu permittis, uolo ego illi beluae ostendere, quando   3
adeo ferox praesultat hostium signis, me ex ea familia ortum
quae Gallorum agmen ex rupe Tarpeia deiecit.' Tum dic-   4
20 tator 'macte uirtute' inquit 'ac pietate in patrem patriamque,
T. Manli, esto. Perge et nomen Romanum inuictum iuuantibus dis praesta.' Armant inde iuuenem aequales; pedestre   5
scutum capit, Hispano cingitur gladio ad propiorem habili
pugnam. Armatum adornatumque aduersus Gallum stolide
25 laetum et—quoniam id quoque memoria dignum antiquis
uisum est—linguam etiam ab inrisu exserentem producunt.
Recipiunt inde se ad stationem; et duo in medio armati   6
spectaculi magis more quam lege belli destituuntur, nequa-
quam uisu ac specie aestimantibus pares. Corpus alteri   7
30 magnitudine eximium, uersicolori ueste pictisque et auro
caelatis refulgens armis; media in altero militaris statura
modicaque in armis habilibus magis quam decoris species;
non cantus, non exsultatio armorumque agitatio uana sed   8
pectus animorum iraeque tacitae plenum; omnem ferociam
35 in discrimen ipsum certaminis distulerat. Vbi constitere   9
inter duas acies tot circa mortalium animis spe metuque
pendentibus, Gallus uelut moles superne imminens proiecto
laeua scuto in aduenientis arma hostis uanum caesim cum
ingenti sonitu ensem deiecit; Romanus mucrone subrecto,   10
40 cum scuto scutum imum perculisset totoque corpore interior

periculo uolneris factus insinuasset se inter corpus armaque,
uno alteroque subinde ictu uentrem atque inguina hausit et
in spatium ingens ruentem porrexit hostem. Iacentis inde 11
corpus ab omni alia uexatione intactum uno torque spoliauit,
45 quem respersum cruore collo circumdedit suo. Defixerat 12
pauor cum admiratione Gallos: Romani alacres ab statione
obuiam militi suo progressi, gratulantes laudantesque ad
dictatorem perducunt. Inter carminum prope in modum incon- 13
dita quaedam militariter ioculantes Torquati cognomen
50 auditum; celebratum deinde posteris etiam familiae honori
fuit. Dictator coronam auream addidit donum mirisque 14
pro contione eam pugnam laudibus tulit.

ꙮ *From the third decade* (*Books 21–30*)
The causes of the Second Punic War, 21.1.1–2.2

In parte operis mei licet mihi praefari, quod in principio **1**
summae totius professi plerique sunt rerum scriptores, bellum
maxime omnium memorabile quae unquam gesta sint, me
scripturum, quod Hannibale duce Carthaginienses cum
5 populo Romano gessere. Nam neque ualidiores opibus ullae 2
inter se ciuitates gentesque contulerunt arma neque his ipsis
tantum unquam uirium aut roboris fuit, et haud ignotas
belli artes inter sese sed expertas primo Punico conserebant
bello, et adeo uaria fortuna belli ancepsque Mars fuit ut
10 propius periculum fuerint qui uicerunt. Odiis etiam prope 3
maioribus certarunt quam uiribus, Romanis indignantibus
quod uictoribus uicti ultro inferrent arma, Poenis, quod
superbe auareque crederent imperitatum uictis esse. Fama 4

est etiam Hannibalem, annorum ferme nouem, pueriliter
15 blandientem patri Hamilcari ut duceretur in Hispaniam, cum
perfecto Africo bello exercitum eo traiecturus sacrificaret,
altaribus admotum tactis sacris iure iurando adactum se cum
primum posset hostem fore populo Romano. Angebant   5
ingentis spiritus uirum Sicilia Sardiniaque amissae: nam et
20 Siciliam nimis celeri desperatione rerum concessam et
Sardiniam inter motum Africae fraude Romanorum, stipendio
etiam insuper imposito, interceptam. His anxius curis ita   **2**
se Africo bello quod fuit sub recentem Romanam pacem,
per quinque annos, ita deinde nouem annis in Hispania
25 augendo Punico imperio gessit ut appareret maius eum quam   2
quod gereret agitare in animo bellum et, si diutius uixisset,
Hamilcare duce Poenos arma Italiae inlaturos fuisse, qui
Hannibalis ductu intulerunt.

Hannibal crosses the Alps, 21.35.4–12

Nono die in iugum Alpium peruentum est per inuia plera-   **35.**4
que et errores, quos aut ducentium fraus aut, ubi fides iis
non esset, temere initae ualles a coniectantibus iter faciebant.
Biduum in iugo statiua habita fessisque labore ac pugnando   5
5 quies data militibus; iumentaque aliquot, quae prolapsa in
rupibus erant, sequendo uestigia agminis in castra peruenere.
Fessis taedio tot malorum niuis etiam casus, occidente iam   6
sidere Vergiliarum, ingentem terrorem adiecit. Per omnia   7
niue oppleta cum signis prima luce motis segniter agmen
10 incederet pigritiaque et desperatio in omnium uoltu emineret,
praegressus signa Hannibal in promunturio quodam, unde   8

longe ac late prospectus erat, consistere iussis militibus
Italiam ostentat subiectosque Alpinis montibus Circum-
padanos campos, moeniaque eos tum transcendere non   9
15 Italiae modo sed etiam urbis Romanae; cetera plana, procliuia fore; uno aut summum altero proelio arcem et caput
Italiae in manu ac potestate habituros. Procedere inde   10
agmen coepit iam nihil ne hostibus quidem praeter parua
furta per occasionem temptantibus. Ceterum iter multo
20 quam in adscensu fuerat—ut pleraque Alpium ab Italia sicut
breuiora ita arrectiora sunt—difficilius fuit; omnis enim   11
ferme uia praeceps, angusta, lubrica erat, ut neque sustinere 12
se ab lapsu possent nec qui paulum titubassent haerere ad-
flicti uestigio suo, aliique super alios et iumenta in homines
25 occiderent.

Scipio addresses his army, 21.40.6–11

'Erit igitur in hoc certamine   **40.**6
is uobis illisque animus qui uictoribus et uictis esse solet.
Nec nunc illi quia audent sed quia necesse est pugnaturi
sunt, qui plures paene perierint quam supersint; nisi cre-   7
5 ditis, qui exercitu incolumi pugnam detractauere, eos duabus
partibus peditum equitumque in transitu Alpium amissis
plus spei nactos esse. At enim pauci quidem sunt sed   8
uigentes animis corporibusque, quorum robora ac uires uix
sustinere uis ulla possit. Effigies immo, umbrae hominum,   9
10 fame, frigore, inluuie, squalore enecti, contusi ac debilitati
inter saxa rupesque; ad hoc praeusti artus, niue rigentes

nerui, membra torrida gelu, quassata fractaque arma, claudi
ac debiles equi. Cum hoc equite, cum hoc pedite pugna-   10
turi estis; reliquias extremas hostis, non hostem habetis, ac
15 nihil magis uereor quam ne cui, uos cum pugnaueritis,
Alpes uicisse Hannibalem uideantur. Sed ita forsitan decuit,   11
cum foederum ruptore duce ac populo deos ipsos sine
ulla humana ope committere ac profligare bellum, nos, qui
secundum deos uiolati sumus, commissum ac profligatum
20 conficere.'

Scipio concludes his speech, 21.41.13–17

'Atque utinam pro decore tantum   **41.**13
hoc uobis et non pro salute esset certamen! Non de pos-   14
sessione Siciliae ac Sardiniae, de quibus quondam agebatur,
sed pro Italia uobis est pugnandum. Nec est alius ab tergo   15
5 exercitus qui, nisi nos uincimus, hosti obsistat, nec Alpes aliae
sunt, quas dum superant, comparari noua possint praesidia;
hic est obstandum, milites, uelut si ante Romana moenia
pugnemus. Vnusquisque se non corpus suum sed coniugem   16
ac liberos paruos armis protegere putet; nec domesticas
10 solum agitet curas sed identidem hoc animo reputet nostras
nunc intueri manus senatum populumque Romanum: qualis   17
nostra uis uirtusque fuerit, talem deinde fortunam illius urbis
ac Romani imperii fore.'

Hannibal illustrates the nature of the situation, 21.42–43.10

Haec apud Romanos consul. Hannibal rebus prius quam   **42**
uerbis adhortandos milites ratus, circumdato ad spectaculum
exercitu captiuos montanos uinctos in medio statuit armisque
Gallicis ante pedes eorum proiectis interrogare interpretem
5 iussit, ecquis, si uinculis leuaretur armaque et equum uictor
acciperet, decertare ferro uellet. Cum ad unum omnes fer-   2
rum pugnamque poscerent et deiecta in id sors esset, se quisque eum optabat quem fortuna in id certamen legeret, et, <ut>   3
cuiusque sors exciderat, alacer, inter gratulantes gaudio ex-
10 sultans, cum sui moris tripudiis arma raptim capiebat. Vbi   4
uero dimicarent, is habitus animorum non inter eiusdem modo
condicionis homines erat sed etiam inter spectantes uolgo,
ut non uincentium magis quam bene morientium fortuna
laudaretur.

Cum sic aliquot spectatis paribus adfectos di-   **43**
15 misisset, contione inde aduocata ita apud eos locutus fertur.
'Si, quem animum in alienae sortis exemplo paulo ante   2
habuistis, eundem mox in aestimanda fortuna uestra habue-
ritis, uicimus, milites; neque enim spectaculum modo illud
sed quaedam ueluti imago uestrae condicionis erat. Ac   3
20 nescio an maiora uincula maioresque necessitates uobis
quam captiuis uestris fortuna circumdederit. Dextra laeua-   4
que duo maria claudunt nullam ne ad effugium quidem
nauem habentes; circa Padus amnis, maior [Padus] ac
uiolentior Rhodano, ab tergo Alpes urgent, uix integris

25   uobis ac uigentibus transitae. Hic uincendum aut morien-   5
dum, milites, est, ubi primum hosti occurristis. Et eadem
fortuna, quae necessitatem pugnandi imposuit, praemia
uobis ea uictoribus proponit quibus ampliora homines ne
ab dis quidem immortalibus optare solent. Si Siciliam   6

30   tantum ac Sardiniam parentibus nostris ereptas nostra uirtute reciperaturi essemus, satis tamen ampla pretia essent:
quidquid Romani tot triumphis partum congestumque pos-
sident, id omne uestrum cum ipsis dominis futurum est; in   7
hanc tam opimam mercedem, agite dum, dis bene iuuantibus

35   arma capite. Satis adhuc in uastis Lusitaniae Celitiberiae-   8
que montibus pecora consectando nullum emolumentum
tot laborum periculorumque uestrorum uidistis; tempus est   9
iam opulenta uos ac ditia stipendia facere et magna operae
pretia mereri, tantum itineris per tot montes fluminaque et

40   tot armatas gentes emensos. Hic uobis terminum laborum   10
fortuna dedit; hic dignam mercedem emeritis stipendiis
dabit.'

Hannibal concludes his speech, 21.44.1–9

'Quocumque circumtuli oculos, plena omnia uideo ani-   **44**
morum ac roboris, ueteranum peditem, generosissimarum
gentium equites frenatos infrenatosque, uos socios fidelis-   2
simos fortissimosque, uos, Carthaginienses, cum <pro> patria,

5   tum ob iram iustissimam pugnaturos. Inferimus bellum   3
infestisque signis descendimus in Italiam, tanto audacius
fortiusque pugnaturi quam hostis, quanto maior spes, maior
est animus inferentis uim quam arcentis. Accendit prae-   4

terea et stimulat animos dolor, iniuria, indignitas. Ad sup-
10 plicium depoposcerunt me ducem primum, deinde uos
omnes qui Saguntum oppugnassetis; deditos ultimis crucia-
tibus adfecturi fuerunt. Crudelissima ac superbissima gens　　　5
sua omnia suique arbitrarii facit; cum quibus bellum, cum quibus pacem habeamus, se modum imponere aequum censet.
15 Circumscribit includitque nos terminis montium fluminumque, quos non excedamus, neque eos, quos statuit, terminos
obseruat: "Ne transieris Hiberum; ne quid rei tibi sit cum　　　6
Saguntinis." Ad Hiberum est Saguntum? "Nusquam te
uestigio moueris." Parum est quod ueterrimas prouincias　　　7
20 meas, Siciliam ac Sardiniam, <ademisti?> Adimis etiam His-
panias, et, inde <si de>cessero, in Africam transcendes. < tran-
scendes> autem? Transcendisse dico. Duos consules huius
anni, unum in Africam, alterum in Hispaniam miserunt.
Nihil usquam nobis relictum est nisi quod armis uindicari-
25 mus. Illis timidis et ignauis esse licet, qui respectum habent,　　　8
quos sua terra, suus ager per tuta ac pacata itinera fugientes
accipient: uobis necesse est fortibus uiris esse et, omnibus
inter uictoriam mortemue certa desperatione abruptis,
aut uincere aut, si fortuna dubitabit, in proelia potius quam
30 in fuga mortem oppetere. Si hoc [bene fixum] omnibus　　　9
destinatum in animo est, iterum dicam, uicistis; nullum
contemptu m<ortis incitamentum> ad uincendum homini ab
dis immortalibus acrius datum est.'

The day after Cannae, 22.51.1–9

Hannibali uictori cum ceteri circumfusi gratularentur **51**
suaderentque ut, tanto perfunctus bello, diei quod reliquum
esset noctisque insequentis quietem et ipse sibi sumeret et
fessis daret militibus, Maharbal praefectus equitum, minime 2
5 cessandum ratus, 'Immo ut quid hac pugna sit actum scias,
die quinto' inquit, 'uictor in Capitolio epulaberis. Sequere;
cum equite, ut prius uenisse quam uenturum sciant, prae-
cedam.' Hannibali nimis laeta res est uisa maiorque quam 3
ut eam statim capere animo posset. Itaque uoluntatem se
10 laudare Maharbalis ait; ad consilium pensandum temporis
opus esse. Tum Maharbal: 'Non omnia nimirum eidem 4
di dedere. Vincere scis, Hannibal; uictoria uti nescis.'
Mora eius diei satis creditur saluti fuisse urbi atque imperio.

15 Postero die ubi primum inluxit, ad spolia legenda foedam- 5
que etiam hostibus spectandam stragem insistunt. Iacebant 6
tot Romanorum milia, pedites passim equitesque, ut quem
cuique fors aut pugna iunxerat aut fuga; adsurgentes quidam
ex strage media cruenti, quos stricta matutino frigore excita-
20 uerant uolnera, ab hoste oppressi sunt; quosdam et iacentes 7
uiuos succisis feminibus poplitibusque inuenerunt, nudantes
ceruicem iugulumque et reliquum sanguinem iubentes hau-
rire; inuenti quidam sunt mersis in effossam terram capitibus 8
quos sibi ipsos fecisse foueas obruentesque ora superiecta
25 humo interclusisse spiritum apparebat. Praecipue conuertit 9
omnes subtractus Numida mortuo superincubanti Romano

uiuus naso auribusque laceratis, cum manibus ad capiendum
telum inutilibus, in rabiem ira uersa laniando dentibus hostem
exspirasset.

⌘ *From the fourth decade* (*Books 31–40*)
The beginning of the Bacchic conspiracy, 39.9.1–7

Huius mali labes ex Etruria Romam ueluti contagione   **9**
morbi penetrauit. Primo magnitudo urbis capacior patien-
tiorque talium malorum ea celauit; tandem indicium hoc
maxime modo ad Postumium consulem peruenit. P. Aebutius,   2
5 cuius pater publico equo stipendia fecerat, pupillus relictus,
mortuis deinde tutoribus sub tutela Duroniae matris et uitrici
T. Semproni Rutili educatus fuerat. Et mater dedita uiro erat,   3
et uitricus, quia tutelam ita gesserat ut rationem reddere non
posset, aut tolli pupillum aut obnoxium sibi uinculo aliquo
10 fieri cupiebat. Via una corruptelae Bacchanalia erant. Mater   4
adulescentulum appellat: se pro aegro eo uouisse, ubi primum
conualuisset, Bacchis eum se initiaturam; damnatam uoti
benignitate deum exsoluere id uelle; decem dierum castimo-
nia opus esse; decimo die cenatum, deinde pure lautum in
15 sacrarium deducturam. Scortum nobile libertina Hispala   5
Faecenia, non digna quaestu cui ancillula adsuerat, etiam
postquam manumissa erat, eodem se genere tuebatur. Huic   6
consuetudo iuxta uicinitatem cum Aebutio fuit, minime
adulescentis aut rei aut famae damnosa; ultro enim amatus
20 adpetitusque erat, et maligne omnia praebentibus suis mere-
triculae munificentia sustinebatur. Quin eo processerat con-   7
suetudine capta ut post patroni mortem, quia in nullius manu

erat, tutore ab tribunis et praetore petito, cum testamentum
faceret unum Aebutium institueret heredem.

The Bacchic conspiracy (continued), 39.10.1–8

Haec amoris pignora cum essent, nec quicquam secretum   **10**
alter ab altero haberent, per iocum adulescens uetat eam
mirari si per aliquot noctes secubuisset: religionis se causa, ut   2
uoto pro ualetudine sua facto liberetur, Bacchis initiari uelle.
5   Id ubi mulier audiuit, perturbata 'Di meliora!' inquit; mori et
sibi et illi satius esse quam id faceret, et in caput eorum
detestari minas periculaque, qui id suasissent. Admiratus cum   3
uerba tum perturbationem tantam adulescens parcere exsecrationibus iubet: matrem id sibi adsentiente uitrico impe-
10   rasse. 'Vitricus ergo' inquit 'tuus (matrem enim insimulare   4
forsitan fas non sit) pudicitiam famam spem uitamque tuam
perditum ire hoc facto properat.' Eo magis mirabundo   5
quaerentique quid rei esset, pacem ueniamque precata
deorum dearumque si coacta caritate eius silenda enuntiasset,
15   ancillam se ait dominae comitem id sacrarium intrasse,
liberam nunquam eo accessisse. Scire corruptelarum omnis   6
generis eam officinam esse, et iam biennio constare neminem
initiatum ibi maiorem annis uiginti. Vt quisque introductus   7
sit, uelut uictimam tradi sacerdotibus; eos deducere in locum
20   qui circumsonet ululatibus cantuque symphoniae et cymba-
lorum et tympanorum pulsu, ne uox quiritantis cum per uim
stuprum inferatur exaudiri possit. Orare inde atque obsecrare   8
ut eam rem quocumque modo discuteret, nec se eo praecipi-
taret, ubi omnia infanda patienda primum, deinde facienda

25 essent. Neque ante dimisit eum quam fidem dedit adulescens
    ab iis sacris se temperaturum.

The magistrates learn of the conspiracy, 39.13.1–14

    Mulier haud dubie, id quod erat, Aebutium indicem   **13**
    arcani rata esse, ad pedes Sulpiciae procidit, et eam primo   2
    orare coepit, ne mulieris libertinae cum amatore sermonem in
    rem non seriam modo sed capitalem etiam uerti uellet; se
5   terrendi eius causa, non quo sciret quicquam, ea locutam
    esse. Hic Postumius accensus ira tum quoque ait eam cum   3
    Aebutio se amatore cauillari credere, non in domo grauissi-
    mae feminae et cum consule loqui. Et Sulpicia attollere
    pauentem, simul illam adhortari, simul iram generi lenire.
10 Tandem confirmata, multum incusata perfidia Aebutii qui   4
    optime de ipso meritae talem gratiam rettulisset, magnum   5
    sibi metum deorum quorum occulta initia enuntiaret,
    maiorem multo dixit hominum esse, qui se indicem manibus
    suis discerpturi essent. Itaque hoc se Sulpiciam, hoc consulem 6
15 orare, ut se extra Italiam aliquo amandarent ubi reliquum
    uitae degere tuto posset. Bono animo esse iubere eam consul,   7
    et sibi curae fore dicere, ut Romae tuto habitaret.

    Tum Hispala originem sacrorum expromit: primo   8
    sacrarium id feminarum fuisse, nec quemquam eo uirum
20 admitti solitum. Tres in anno statos dies habuisse, quibus
    interdiu Bacchis initiarentur; sacerdotes in uicem matronas
    creari solitas. Pacullam Anniam Campanam sacerdotem   9
    omnia tamquam deum monitu immutasse; nam et uiros
    eam primam filios suos initiasse, Minium et Herennium

25 Cerrinios, et nocturnum sacrum ex diurno, et pro tribus in
   anno diebus quinos singulis mensibus dies initiorum fecisse.
   Ex quo in promiscuo sacra sint et permixti uiri feminis, et   10
   noctis licentia accesserit, nihil ibi facinoris, nihil flagitii
   praetermissum. Plura uirorum inter sese quam feminarum
30 stupra esse; si qui minus patientes dedecoris sint et pigriores   11
   ad facinus, pro uictimis immolari. Nihil nefas ducere, hanc
   summam inter eos religionem esse. Viros uelut mente capta   12
   cum iactatione fanatica corporis uaticinari; matronas Baccharum habitu crinibus sparsis cum ardentibus facibus decur-
35 rere ad Tiberim, demissasque in aquam faces, quia uiuum
   sulpur cum calce insit, integra flamma efferre. Raptos a dis   13
   homines dici quos machinae inligatos ex conspectu in abditos
   specus abripiant; eos esse qui aut coniurare aut sociari
   facinoribus aut stuprum pati noluerint. Multitudinem ingen-   14
40 tem, alterum iam prope populum esse, in iis nobiles quosdam
   uiros feminasque. Biennio proximo institutum esse ne quis
   maior uiginti annis initiaretur; captari aetates et erroris et
   stupri patientes.

The consul's speech, 39.15.1–14

   Ad haec officia dimissis magistratibus, consules in rostra   **15**
   escenderunt, et contione aduocata, cum sollemne carmen
   precationis, quod praefari solent priusquam populum adlo-
   quantur magistratus, peregisset consul, ita coepit. 'Nulli   2
5 umquam contioni, Quirites, tam non solum apta sed etiam
   necessaria haec sollemnis deorum comprecatio fuit, quae uos
   admoneret hos esse deos, quos colere uenerari precarique

maiores uestri instituissent, non illos, qui prauis et externis   3

religionibus captas mentes uelut furialibus stimulis ad omne

10 scelus et ad omnem libidinem agerent. Equidem nec quid   4

taceam nec quatenus proloquar inuenio. Si aliquid ignorabi-

tis, ne locum neglegentiae dem, si omnia nudauero, ne

nimium terroris offundam uobis uereor. Quidquid dixero,   5

minus quam pro atrocitate et magnitudine rei dictum scitote

15 esse; ut ad cauendum satis sit, dabitur opera a nobis.

'Bacchanalia tota iam pridem Italia et nunc per urbem   6

etiam multis locis esse, non fama modo accepisse uos, sed

crepitibus etiam ululatibusque nocturnis qui personant tota

urbe, certum habeo, ceterum quae ea res sit, ignorare; alios   7

20 deorum aliquem cultum, alios concessum ludum et lasciuiam

credere esse, et qualecumque sit ad paucos pertinere. Quod   8

ad multitudinem eorum attinet, si dixero multa milia homi-

num esse, ilico necesse est exterreamini, nisi adiunxero qui

qualesque sint. Primum igitur mulierum magna pars est, et is   9

25 fons mali huiusce fuit; deinde simillimi feminis mares, stuprati

et constupratores fanatici, uigiliis uino strepitibus clamoribus-

que nocturnis attoniti. Nullas adhuc uires coniuratio, ceterum   10

incrementum ingens uirium habet, quod in dies plures fiunt.

Maiores uestri ne uos quidem, nisi cum aut uexillo in arce   11

30 posito comitiorum causa exercitus eductus esset, aut plebi

concilium tribuni edixissent, aut aliquis ex magistratibus ad

contionem uocasset, forte temere coire uoluerunt; et

ubicumque multitudo esset, ibi et legitimum rectorem multi-

tudinis censebant debere esse. Quales primum nocturnos   12

35 coetus, deinde promiscuos mulierum ac uirorum esse creditis?

Si quibus aetatibus initientur mares sciatis, non misereat uos   13
eorum solum, sed etiam pudeat. Hoc sacramento initiatos
iuuenes milites faciendos censetis, Quirites? His ex obsceno
sacrario eductis arma committenda? Hi cooperti stupris suis   14
40 alienisque pro pudicitia coniugum ac liberorum uestrorum
ferro decernent?

The consul's speech (continued), 39.16.1–13

'Minus tamen esset, si flagitiis tantum effeminati forent   **16**
(ipsorum id magna ex parte dedecus erat), <et> a facinoribus
manus, mentem a fraudibus abstinuissent; numquam tantum   2
malum in re publica fuit, nec ad plures nec ad plura pertinens.
5 Quidquid his annis libidine, quidquid fraude, quidquid
scelere peccatum est, ex illo uno sacrario scitote ortum esse.
Necdum omnia, in quae coniurarunt edita facinora habent.   3
Adhuc priuatis noxiis, quia nondum ad rem publicam
opprimendam satis uirium est, coniuratio sese impia tenet.
10 Crescit et serpit cotidie malum. Iam maius est quam ut capere
id priuata fortuna possit; ad summam rem publicam spectat.
Nisi praecauetis, Quirites, iam huic diurnae legitime ab   4
consule uocatae par nocturna contio esse poterit. Nunc illi
uos singuli uniuersos contionantes timent. Iam ubi uos dilapsi
15 domos et in rura uestra eritis, illi coierint, consultabunt de sua
salute simul ac uestra pernicie; tum singulis uobis uniuersi
timendi erunt. Optare igitur unusquisque uestrum debet ut   5
bona mens suis omnibus fuerit; si quem libido, <si> furor in
illum gurgitem abripuit, illorum eum cum quibus in omne
20 flagitium et facinus coniurauit, non suum iudicet.

'Ne quis etiam errore labatur uestrum, Quirites, non sum   6
securus. Nihil enim in speciem fallacius est quam praua
religio. Vbi deorum numen praetenditur sceleribus, subit   7
animum timor ne fraudibus humanis uindicandis diuini
25 iuris aliquid immixtum uiolemus. Hac uos religione innume-
rabilia decreta pontificum, senatus consulta, haruspicum
denique responsa liberant. Quotiens hoc patrum auorumque   8
aetate magistratibus negotium est datum uti sacra externa fieri
uetarent, sacrificulos uatesque foro circo urbe prohiberent,
30 uaticinos libros conquirerent comburerentque, omnem disci-
plinam sacrificandi praeterquam more Romano abolerent!   9
Iudicabant enim prudentissimi uiri omnis diuini humanique
iuris nihil aeque dissoluendae religionis esse quam ubi non
35 patrio sed externo ritu sacrificaretur.

'Haec uobis praedicenda ratus sum ne qua superstitio   10
agitaret animos uestros cum demolientes nos Bacchanalia
discutientesque nefarios coetus cerneretis. Omnia diis propitiis 11
uolentibusque [ea] faciemus, qui quia suum numen sceleribus
40 libidinibusque contaminari indigne ferebant, ex occultis ea
tenebris in lucem extraxerunt, nec patefieri ut impunita
essent, sed ut uindicarentur et opprimerentur uoluerunt.   12
Senatus quaestionem extra ordinem de ea re mihi conlegae-
que meo mandauit. Nos quae ipsis nobis agenda sunt impigre
45 exsequemur; uigiliarum nocturnarum curam per urbem
minoribus magistratibus mandauimus. Vos quoque aequum   13
est quae uestra munia sunt, quo quisque loco positus erit,
quod imperabitur, impigre praestare, et dare operam ne quid
fraude noxiorum periculi aut tumultus oriatur.'

Commentary

∾ *From Livy's preface*
Praef. 6–10

Ancient historians generally preface their works with discussions of their subject, approach, and position relative to those of other historians, and they do so in language that repays close scrutiny. In the first part of his preface, Livy expresses doubt about his ability to achieve a result worth the effort of writing Rome's history from the beginning: the task is enormous and many others have done it before him. Still the project will allow him to turn his attention away from the evils of the present to the virtues of the past. In the passage discussed below, Livy writes that he will not argue about the truth or falsehood of the oldest stories about Rome; rather the reward of studying history is a clear view of examples of good and bad conduct and thus of the impact of morality on events. The metaphors that Livy uses in this passage deserve attention, because they introduce themes that reappear throughout his work.

1–3   **quae . . . traduntur** the rel. clause placed before its antecedent, *ea* (line 3)

       ante conditam condendamue urbem "before the city was founded or about to be founded"

       poeticis magis . . . fabulis . . . incorruptis rerum gestarum monumentis dats., with *decora*, "suitable." The contrast is between the spoken (*fabula*) and written or built (*monumenta*), as well as between poetry and history.

       rerum gestarum cf. the title of Augustus' catalog of achievements, *Res Gestae*

3–4   **in animo est** sc. *mihi*: "I intend"

datur The verb is at the beginning for emphasis.

4–5 **ut . . . faciat** a result clause. The (unexpressed) subject of *faciat* is *antiquitas*.

miscendo gerund with direct object *humana*, "things human"

diuinis neuter: "things divine"

primordia beginnings, origin, or source; Lucretius, *de Rerum Natura* 1.55, says that he will disclose *rerum primordia*, "the origins of things"

augustiora Livy uses the adj. of gods in contrast to humans.

cui = *alicui*

6 **licere** with dat., *cui populo*, and infinitive

oportet impers.

7 **referre** sc. *eas origines*

ea . . . gloria "such is the glory"

populo Romano possessive dat.

7–8 **cum . . . ferat** the subject is *populus Romanus*; translate *ferat* as "claims."

suum modifies *parentem*, and is parallel to *conditorisque sui*

Martem Mars was an important Italian god. Much of his my-thology is derived from that of the Greek warrior-god, Ares, but he also protected crops. The Elder Cato's treatise on farm-ing contains instructions for an agricultural ritual celebrat-ing him (*De Agri Cultura*, 141). At Rome he was honored in cults tied to the urban landscape, such as that of the Salii, who processed through the city bearing shields (one said to have fallen from the sky as a gift from Jupiter, the others, decoys) and stopped at specific places to perform a ritual dance.

potissimum adv. "especially," "above all"

9 **tam . . . quam** correlatives

et hoc "even this"

gentes humanae subject of both *patiantur* and *patiuntur*

9–10 **patiantur . . . patiuntur** the subjunctive indicating a

hypothetical situation, followed by an indicative representing
the actual one

10   **haec et his similia** "these things and things similar to them."
        The prons. refer back to *quae . . . traduntur.*

11–12   **haud** with *magno. Haud* usually qualifies adjs. and advs.

        in magno . . . ponam discrimine *ponere in* + abl., "to regard
        as consisting or comprised (in)" (*OLD* s.v. *ponere*, 24). Trans-
        late as "regard as of no great difference."

        ad illa *illa* points ahead to a series of indirect questions.

        mihi a dat. of reference, which here shows the interest felt by
        the speaker

12–19   After the main clause (*ad illa . . . intendat animum*) the rest
        of this sentence falls into two parts, which convey Rome's
        growth and decline. The first is a series of indirect questions
        (*quae uita, qui mores fuerint, per quos uiros quibusque arti-
        bus . . .*). Livy uses asyndeton (absence of connectives) and
        anaphora (repetition of the same word, here the rel. pron.) at
        the beginning of clauses: *quae . . . qui, per quos, quibus.* Note
        also the increasing length and complexity of those clauses.

13   **intendat** hortary subjunctive

        uita private life, as opposed to *mores*, "public morals"

14   **domi militiaeque** the first appearance in Livy of a common
        phrase encompassing the two spheres of Roman government,
        "at home and at war"

15   **labante . . . disciplina** abl. absolute

        deinde the adv. here connects the second half of the sentence,
        on decline, to the first, on growth, by connecting the two in-
        tellectual acts that Livy wants his reader to perform: *intendat
        animum . . . deinde . . . sequatur animo.*

16   **uelut dissidentes primo mores sequatur animo** sc. *quisque*
        as subject of *sequatur*

        primo "at first." This clears the way for the *deinde* and *tum*
        that follow.

sequatur animo "let him follow in thought"

16–17   **deinde ut . . . lapsi sint . . .** [sc. *mores*]: more indirect questions

praecipites the speed of collapse increases

18–19   **donec** until; *donec* + pf. is frequent in Livy

remedia The metaphor changes to one of medicine. The nature of the cure is left unspecified.

peruentum est impers. construction. Translate by taking the person from *possumus*: "we have arrived." The metaphorical language conveys the idea of physical disintegration and collapse (*labante . . . dissidentes . . . lapsi sint . . . ire coeperint praecipites*), the increasing rate of deterioration (*paulatim . . . magis magisque . . . ire coeperint praecipites*), and how collapsing morals bring down the empire with them.

19–20   **hoc illud est** "it is this that is"

in cognitione rerum a way of saying "in the study of history"

salubre This continues the medical metaphor.

frugiferum literally "fruit-bearing"; one can translate it as "profitable," but it is good to keep in mind the idea of fruitfulness as an adjunct to health.

omnis emphatic by position

exempli here, a specimen of conduct. This is an important word for Roman historians, since it can mean both a specimen of conduct and a specimen of conduct used as an illustration or proof.

21   **documenta** examples serving as precedents

monumento a reminder, a record, a monument, a written history

in inlustri posita monumento This can be translated in ways that bring the metaphors into play to greater or lesser degrees, ranging from "expressed in a clear record" to "set up on a monument bathed in light."

21–22   **tibi tuaeque rei publicae** Livy collars his readers, individually, and lets them know that he expects them to use what they learn from the *AUC* for the public good. The combination of "you" and "your republic" responds to the expression of public and private morals in *quae uita qui mores fuerint.*

quod imitere (= *imiteris*): rel. clause of characteristic

23   **inceptu/exitu** abl. of respect

quod uites another rel. clause of characteristic

∾ *From the first decade* (*Books 1–10*)
The founding of Rome, 1.6.3–7.3

The relationship between the twins Romulus and Remus turned ugly when their desire to found a city (*cupido . . . urbis condendae*) gave way to the desire to rule (*regni cupido*). Livy reports two versions of the killing of Remus and calls each a tradition (*fertur / fama est*). The second demonstrates how Romulus chose his city over his brother, thus making patriotic fratricide part of Rome from its foundation.

1   **Numitori** the grandfather of Romulus and Remus, who had been driven from the throne of Alba Longa by his brother, Amulius

Albana re "the rule at Alba." Alba Longa was in Latium, about twelve miles from the site of Rome.

2   **cupido** "passionate desire" plays an important role in this story

3   **urbis condendae** "of founding a city," an objective gen. of the gerundive construction

Et "and in fact"

supererat multitudo the usual reason for sending forth a colony

4–5   **ad id** "and in addition to these"

qui . . . facerent best translated as a result clause

spem + acc. and infinitive expressing the nature of the hope or expectation

paruam Albam, paruum Lauinium, the predicate adjs. (adjs. that denote something said about their subject, e.g., "Alba would be small") gain further emphasis from the anaphora

6   **fore** = *futurum esse*

     prae + abl. "in comparison to"

     quae conderetur part of the expectation (*spes*), thus a subordi-
     nate clause in indirect speech, with its verb in the subjunctive

     interuenit the position of the verb makes it emphatic

7   **cogitationibus** the thoughts of future greatness

     regni cupido in apposition to *auitum malum*; *regni* is an ob-
     jective gen.

8–10 **Quoniam . . . essent nec . . . posset** causal clauses

     aetatis uerecundia "the deference of youth"

10–11 **ut di . . . legerent** purpose after *capiunt*

     tutelae gen.

     auguriis "by means of bird-omens"

     qui . . . daret, qui . . . regeret indirect questions after *legerent*

12   **Palatium Romulus, Remus Auentinum** chiastic wordorder.
     The Palatine was the central and traditionally oldest hill of
     Rome; it overlooked the city's earliest commercial area, the fo-
     rum Boarium, as well as the old crossing points of the Tiber and
     the paths along the riverbank. At its base was the Lupercal, the
     cave where the she-wolf was said to have suckled the exposed
     twins. During the republican period the Palatine became a fash-
     ionable neighborhood: Cicero lived there, as did Crassus, Milo,
     and Mark Antony. Augustus build his house there, as well as
     the Temple of Apollo Palatinus, vowed in 36 BCE, completed in
     28 BCE, and thus under construction about the time when Livy
     wrote these books. The Aventine is the southernmost of the ca-
     nonical seven hills of Rome. During the republic it was a plebe-
     ian stronghold; and it was outside the pomerium until 49 CE.

     ad inaugurandum "for taking the auspices," that is, taking
     omens by watching the flight of birds

13   **templa** predicate acc., after *Palatium* and *Auentinum*, the ob-
     jects of *capiunt*. A *templum* was a space marked out for the
     taking of auspices.

14   **Priori** here "first" (of the two brothers). *Primo* would suggest that Remus was the first person ever to receive a bird sign.

     uenisse + dat. "to have happened to" (*OLD* s.v. *uenire*, 15)

     sex uoltures in apposition to *augurium*

15-16   **cum . . . ostendisset** *cum* temporal in a subordinate clause in indirect speech

     consalutauerat plpf., because it reports what happened before *uertuntur*

17   **tempore . . . praecepto** literally, "the moment (sc. of the birds) having been seized first" (in contrast to *numero*)

     illi . . . hi "the supporters of Remus . . . those of Romulus"

17-18   **regnum trahebant** "sought to claim," the English does not keep the metaphor in *traho* of a tug-of-war over the kingship

18   **cum altercatione congressi** "having come together in a dispute"

     certamine abl. of cause

19   **ibi** "thereupon"

20   **ludibrio fratris** dat. of purpose followed by an objective gen.

20-21   **nouos transiluisse muros** an act of arrogance and a threat to the new city's physical and religious integrity

     irato predicate position, "by a Romulus who was *angry*"

21-23   **cum uerbis quoque increpitans adiecisset** draws attention to the direct speech that follows, the first made by a character in Livy

     'Sic deinde . . . mea' With these words Romulus recasts his murder of his brother into an act of patriotism. There is an ellipse of a verb expressing the thought "I shall kill" or "he shall die."

     solus . . . Romulus the emphasis here is on *solus*

     potitus [sc. *est*] + abl.

24   **condita . . . conditoris** the repetition drives home the important points: this is the founding of the city, and its founder is Romulus. Cf. also line 11, above.

Horatius at the bridge, 2.10.1–13

At the end of Book 1, the Romans expelled the family of the Etruscan kings, the Tarquins, and established a republic led by consuls,
whose power was limited, partly because there were two of them,
and partly because they were elected annually. The Tarquins took
refuge with Lars Porsenna, the ruler of Clusium, a major Etruscan
city northeast of Rome. Persuaded by the Tarquins, Porsenna attacked Rome. Having captured the Janiculum, he prepared to send
his army across the Tiber, in order to strike at the heart of the city.
Livy tells here the story of Horatius Cocles, the man who saved
Rome at this critical moment.

1 **cum . . . adessent** narrative (i.e., circumstantial) *cum*

   pro se quisque "each acting on his own behalf"; the sing. of
   quisque can be used, as here, to distribute a pl. subject.

2 **demigrant . . . saepiunt** historical presents, used for vividness

   urbem ipsam used here in contrast with *in urbem* to form a
   transition: "as for the city itself" (*OLD* s.v. *urbs*, 3)

   alia . . . alia n. pls. "some [sc. places] . . . others"

3 **Tiberi** *Tiberis, -is*, m. (f.) the Tiber river (acc. *-im*; abl. *-i*)

   Tiberi obiecto a common topographical use of the pass. *obi-
   ectus*, "to be in the way" or "to constitute a defense"

   pons sublicius The bridge connecting Rome (at the forum Boari-
   um) to the Janiculum. According to legend it was originally built
   by the fourth king of Rome, Ancus Marcius (Livy 1.33.6), and
   received its name from the word *sublica* (pile). The bridge was
   made entirely of wood, apparently for religious reasons; its care
   was the concern of the college of pontifices (lit. "bridge-makers"
   Varro, *De Lingua Latina*, 5.83). It was frequently destroyed but
   always restored, and still standing in the fourth century CE. (See
   Richardson, *A New Topgraphical Dictionary*.)

   iter with *dare*, "to grant passage"

4 **ni . . . fuisset** the apodosis of a past contrafactual condition; *ni*
   for *nisi* is an archaism.

unus uir "one man" single-handedly saves Rome. This the first instance of an expression that appears repeatedly in Livy. Other saviors of Rome honored with it are M. Manlius, who saves the citadel from the Gauls at 5.47.4, Camillus, at 6.23.5, and Fabius Maximus, at 30.26.9. Note, however, that while one man saves the day conspicuously, many anonymous others are busy chopping away at the bridge.

Horatius Cocles Cocles "one-eyed," apparently from the Greek Κύκλυψ (*OLD*). See also Varro, *De Lingua Latina* 7.71: *ab oculo cocles, ut ocles, dictus, qui unum haberet oculum.*

5   **id munimentum** The pron. refers to Horatius, but has been drawn into the gender of *munimentum*; the metaphor links him to Rome's other defenses: the walls and the river.

fortuna urbis Romae the originally Hellenistic idea of a city's fortune (τύχη)

6   **Qui** connective rel., = *et is*

in statione pontis *in statione* "on guard," "at one's post," here with *pontis* as a defining gen.: "at his post, namely, the bridge"

captum [*esse*]; parallel to *decurrere* and *relinquere*

7   **Ianiculum** the Janiculum, a ridge on the right bank of the Tiber

8   **suorum** here substantive: "of his own men"

9   **obsistens** sc. *eis*

deum gen. pl., depending, with *hominum*, on *fidem*

10   **testabatur** introduces the indirect statement that follows. Horatius' words show him to be both a brave soldier and a fine rhetorician. Most of Livy's heroes are skilled at persuasive speech. The idea that a hero should be able both to speak well and accomplish great deeds is as old as the Homeric poems.

nequiquam in an emphatic postition

11-12   **si . . . reliquissent . . . plus hostium . . . fore** a fut. more vivid condition in indirect statement in secondary sequence; direct speech would give *nequiquam vos fugitis*; *si . . . reliqueris . . . plus hostium erunt.*

a tergo "behind them"

iam "presently"

hostium partitive gen., with *plus*

Palatio Capitolioque the two central hills of Rome

13–15 **Itaque monere, praedicere** The direct expression would be "'And so I exhort, I advise that you ...'" The sentence that follows is also subordinate to *testabatur*.

ut ... interrumpant indirect command

ferro, igni, quacumque ui possint The third element in the list is the broadest: "with iron, with fire, with whatever force they might."

quantum adv.

15 **excepturum** [sc. *esse*]

16–17 **primum aditum** "the nearest part of the approach"

conspecta (w. *terga*), here, "visible to view"

cedentium pugnae *cedo* + dat.

17–18 **ad ineundum proelium** gerundive expressing purpose

ipso miraculo audaciae "by the very wonder of his daring." *Audaciae* is a defining or descriptive gen.

19–20 **Duos** emphatic world order

Sp. Larcium Sp. = Spurius; Larcius is an Etruscan name

T. Herminium T. = Titus; Herminius is an Etruscan name

genere factisque causal abls.

21 **quod tumultuosissimum pugnae erat** *pugna* is a partitive gen., "the most uproarious part of the fight"

23 **exigua parte pontis relicta** abl. absolute

reuocantibus qui rescindebant *reuocantibis* [*illis*] *qui rescindebant*; abl. absolute

24 **coegit** sc. *Horatius*

25–26 **circumferens ... oculos** a poetic expression; with *ad proceres* cf. (of Niobe) *oculos circumtulit alta superbos* ("standing tall, she turned her arrogant gaze"), Ovid, *Met.* 6.169.

proceres Etruscorum "the leading men of the Etruscans." The word *proceres* strengthens the contrast with Cocles, unknown until this deed.

prouocare . . . increpare historical infinitives

26–27   **suae liberatatis** *suae* as opposed to *alienam*

oppugnatum uenire supine with a verb of motion; *uenire* is infinitive in indirect speech introduced by *increpare*.

27–35   **cunctati . . . sustinuit** N.B. the many temporal expressions, *aliquamdiu . . . dum . . . deinde . . .* ; *iam . . . cum simul . . . simul . . .* , in addition to *cunctati, alacritate,* and *subito.*

28–29   **dum . . . circumspectant** *dum* with the pres. indicative denotes continued action in past time.

alius alium "one . . . another"

ut proelium incipiant clause depending on *circumspectant*

30   **Quae** connective rel.

34   **alacritate** causal abl.

perfecti operis the *ab urbe condita* construction, in which the pple. has substantive force: "of the completion of the work"

35–36   **'Tiberine Pater'** the language of prayer and poetry: cf. Ennius, *Ann.* 54: *pater Tiberine tuo cum flumine sancto* ("father Tiber with your sacred stream"); and Vergil, *Aen.* 8.72–73: *'Tuque, o Thybri tuo genitor cum flumine sancto,/ accipite Aenean'* ("and you, O father Tiber, with your sacred stream, receive Aeneas").

36–37   **hunc militem** a poetic way of saying *me*

accipias subjunctive in an object clause after *precor*

ita sic the adv. *ita* connects the sentence to the previous. Translate *sic* with *armatus*: "and thus it came about that, in armor, as he was . . . "

38   **multis superincidentibus telis** abl. absolute

incolumis In other versions of the story (e.g., Polybius 6.55.1–4) Horatius is wounded or dies. Livy has told the story so as to reward good completely.

39-40　**rem** here "a deed" in the same sense as *res gestae*, "accomplishments"

　　　　fidei "credibility"

　　　　ad posteros "among future generations"

　　　　Grata with *ciuitas*; note its emphatic position.

　　　　erga + acc. here, "in return for"

41　　　**statua in comitio** The origins of the story of Horatius are obscure: it may be an aetiology explaining a particular statue identified with Horatius Cocles that once stood in the *comitium*. The *comitium* was the earliest place of public assembly in Rome; it was an inaugurated area, a *templum*, in front of the Curia Hostilia, between the Curia and the Forum Romanum.

　　　　agri partitive gen. with *quantum*

43-44　**pro domesticis copiis** "in proportion to their household supplies"

　　　　ei indirect object of *contulit*

　　　　fraudans *fraudare* means "to cheat or swindle out of," with an abl. of separation

Mucius Scaevola, 2.12.1–16

Horatius Cocles has, as it were, stepped offstage, never to reappear in what survives of Livy's history. He has, however, provided an enduring example of courage and fortitude both to readers and to audiences within the text. His initial attack thwarted, Lars Porsenna establishes a garrison on the Janiculum, sets up his camp near the Tiber, and attempts to starve the city into submission. As the siege continues and Rome's situation grows dire, another Roman steps forth to save the day. This time it is a well-born youth, G. Mucius. The figures change but the setting is constant, for once again the Tiber plays a central role in a fundamental story of Roman heroism.

1-2　　**obsidio erat . . . et . . . inopia** both nom. The gen. *frumenti* depends on *caritate*.

nihilo minus "none the less"

2 **sedendo** abl. of means

expugnaturum se sc. *esse*; indirect statement introduced by *spem Porsenna habebat*

3 **cum** introduces the clause whose main verb is *constituit* (line 9). Note how the impf. indicatives *erat* and *habebat* set the scene and *cum . . . constituit* denotes an abrupt event. This use of *cum* is called *cum-inversum*.

4 **indignum uidebatur** introduces indirect statement: *populum Romanum* is the subject of *obsessum esse* and *eundem populum* that of *obsideri*. Note the emphatic antithesis of *seruientem* vs. *liberum* (line 6).

4-5 **cum sub regibus esset** *cum*-circumstantial clause explaining *seruientem*

7 **fuderit** subject is *populus Romanus*

7-8 **magno audacique aliquo facinore** abl. of means. The word order places emphasis on the adjs.: greatness and daring are Mucius' primary thoughts.

ratus "thinking" introduces indirect statement: *eam indignitatem uindicandam* [*esse*] "that the humiliation should be avenged"

primo adv. in contrast with *dein* (line 9)

9 **constituit** main verb of the first part of the sentence; it completes the syntactical structure begun at line 1; but note how the temporal advs. *primo . . . dein* bridge the break between the two syntatically complete parts of the sentence.

10-11 **ne . . . retraheretur** clause of fearing

consulum iniussu "without the command of the consuls"

12 **fortuna . . . adfirmante** abl. absolute

13-15 **'Transire Tiberim'** Mucius' direct speech makes the scene all the more vivid.

populationum objective gen. (of the wrong avenged) depending on *ultor*

in uicem = *inuicem*, adv. "in exchange," "in turn"

maius placed for emphasis before the parenthetical *si di iuuant*

16 **Adprobant ... proficiscitur** the two short sentences move the action along briskly

17 **Vbi ... uenit** temporal clause

19 **pari fere ornatu** descriptive abl., "with almost equal adornment"

20 **<-que>** *-que* was added by an editor (Aldus) in the early sixteenth century

uolgo adv. "in a mass"

20–21 **uter Porsenna esset** indirect question depending on *sciscitari*, which is itself an infinitive complementing *timens*. Different manuscripts—and editions—of Livy's history spell the Etruscan king's name differently. There is ancient evidence for both *Porsenna* and *Porsinna*.

semet an intensified form of *se*

ignorando regem note the gerund with the direct object, which emphasizes the action

ne ... aperiret clause of fearing after *timens*

semet ipse aperiret quis esset *se* is the direct object of *aperiret*, which introduces the indirect question *quis esset*.

quo rel. adv. "where"

22 **pro rege** "mistaking him for the king"

23 **Vadentem** sc. *Mucium*

qua rel. adv. "by which route," "where"

cruento mucrone abl. of means

24 **ad clamorem** "in response to the cry"

25 **satellites** *satelles*, a word probably Etruscan in origin. It means "bodyguard," or "henchman," often in a contemptous sense.

26 **destitutus** from *destituo*, here in the sense of "abandoned," "left isolated"

27 **metuendus magis quam metuens** "more to be feared than fearing." Note the alliteration.

Romanus in an emphatic position; *civis*, delayed to the end, is also emphatic.

28   **Hostis hostem** The word order emphasizes the person-to-person nature of the conflict.

30   **fortia** direct object of both *facere* and *pati*

31   **idem petentium decus** gen. *petentium* [sc. *iuuenum*] depends on *ordo*; *idem . . . decus* is the direct object of *petentium*.

32-33   **hoc discrimen** looks forward to *ut . . . dimices*

accingere imperative

in singulas horas "hour by hour"

capite . . . tuo Ogilvie, finding no parallels for the simple abl., wants to add *de* (*de capite tuo*).

35   **timueris** jussive subjunctive

37   **circumdari** infinitive with *iuberet*

minitabundus the suffix -*bundus* appears in verbal adjs. with an active force (they can take direct objects)

38   **propere** adv.

quas . . . minas . . . iaceret indirect question

per ambages "through evasive speech"

39   **en tibi** an ethical dat.: "look you"

iis dat. of the person judging

40-41   **accenso . . . foculo** dat. with *inicit*

ad sacrificium *ad* here expresses purpose

Quam a connective rel., direct object of *torreret*

44   **hostilia** "characteristic of an enemy," here n. pl. as a substantive

45-46   **Iuberem . . . staret** pres. contrafactual condition

48   **apud te** "in your mind"

48-49   **ut . . . tuleris** a purpose clause

beneficio in contrast to *minis*

nequisti sc. *ferre*

50   **ut ... grassaremur** objective clause depending on *coniuraui-*
        mus. grassor here, "to go to work," "proceed," in a specific
        manner, with the idea of violence implied

51   **ut cuiusque ceciderit primi** [sc. *sors*] "as each man's lot falls
        out"

52   **quoad te opportunum fortuna dederit** "until fortune leaves
        you exposed"

Cloelia, 2.13.6–11

Lars Porsenna released Mucius, who received the cognomen Scaevola
("Left-handed") because of the loss of his right hand. Impressed by
his courage, Porsinna agreed to a negotiated peace and an exchange
of hostages. Among those handed over by the Romans was a group of
young women, one of whom, Cloelia, led her companions to freedom
by eluding the guards and swimming across the Tiber. Expressions
of courage have come from the previously unknown Horatius Cocles
and the well-born Mucius; now they come from a woman. For a third
time the Tiber provides the setting. The prominent role of the river
and the repeated references to Romans crossing it connect the Janiculum more closely to the core of the city on the other side.

2   **publica** In the emphatic position, this adj. suggests that the
        decora ("honourable achievements" or "exploits") of Roman
        women are usually confined to private life.

        Cloelia a Latin gentile name, also spelled *Cluilia*

4   **procul** usually an adv., but here prep.+ abl.

4–5   **dux agminis uirginum** each gen. depends on the noun before
        it. The first is a possessive gen.; the second a gen. of mate-
        rial. In Livy's eyes Cloelia plays a man's part. Cf. Vergil, *Aen.*
        1.364 (on Dido): *dux femina facti* ("a woman was leader of the
        deed").

        Tiberim tranauit cf. Vergil, *Aen.* 8.651 (on the shield): *et*
        fluuium uinclis innaret Cloelia ruptis ("and Cloelia swimming
        the river, her chains broken").

6   **Romam ad propinquos** "restored them to Rome and their families"

Quod connective rel.; note its position outside the *cum*-clause of which it is the subject

8   **misit** (sc. *rex*)

8–9   **alias . . . facere** *alias* [sc. *uirgines*] indirect statement introduced by the idea of sending *oratores* ("envoys") to demand Cloelia's return; *magni* gen. expressing price, value

uersus with *in* + acc.; the pass. here expresses a middle sense: to cause himself to pass into a new frame of mind

9–10   **supra** prep. + acc. in a position of superiority to

Coclites Muciosque the pls. give a broad force to Porsenna's declaration

dicere historical infinitive

10–13   **prae se ferre** historical infinitive, "positively to affirm." What follows is a pair of fut. more vivid conditions introduced by *prae se ferre*, giving the alternatives:

1) *quemadmodum si non dedatur obses . . . se habiturum* and 2) *sic deditam . . . remissurum*, in which *quemadmodum* "while" is parallel to *sic* "at the same time," *si non dedatur obses* is parallel to *deditam*, and *pro rupto foedus se habiturum* is parallel to *<intactam> inuiolatamque ad suos remissurum*

12   **<intactam> inuiolatamque** Ogilvie's text prints that of the editor Johannes Froben's 1531 Basle edition on the grounds, as he says in his commentary, that if the *–que* after *inuiolatum* is allowed to stand, an adj. must have dropped out.

13   **Vtrimque constitit fides** "the bargain stood on both sides"

14–15   **non tuta solum sed honorata etiam uirtus fuit** note the emphatic position of *tuta* and *honorata*; unemphatic word order would be *non solum tuta sed etiam honorata*

16   **donare** acc. of recipient, abl. of gift (as also in 21–22, below)

16–17   **ipsa quos uellet legeret** "she might choose whom she wished," the subjunctives loosely connected to *dixit*

18   **uirginitati** here, the condition of being a girl of marriageable age

19   **probabile** The young boys (*impubes*) were most vulnerable to
      sexual violation (defined elsewhere as *muliebria pati*).

      aetatem here, an age group

21   **nouam in femina uirtutem ... nouo genere honoris** Note the
      emphatic repetition of the adj.

22–23 **summa Sacra uia** a prestigious place. It was also the location
      of the Temple of the Lares, the house of the *rex sacrorum* and
      the Temple of Jupiter Stator.

      fuit posita The statue was destroyed by 30BC, but replaced.

      uirgo insidens equo The equestrian statue, a Greek type, did
      not appear in Rome before the fourth century. This story,
      then, some versions of which have Cloelia escaping on horse-
      back, and some of which even call her by a different name,
      Valeria, must have come into being as an explanation of a
      fourth-century or later equestrian statue.

Manlius and the Gaul, 7.9.6–10.14

The year is 361 BCE. The setting is the banks of the river Anio, a mere
three miles up the Via Saleria from Rome. In 390 BCE (by Roman reckoning), the Gauls had captured Rome and destroyed much of the city,
all except the citadel (*arx*) on the Capitoline—according to Livy, who
relates the events in the last half of Book 5. (Other sources report that
even the citadel was captured.) The great M. Furius Camillus, who
returned from exile and was appointed dictator, saved the city. He in-
tervened when the Romans were about to pay ransom, drove the Gauls
out of Rome itself, and routed them eight miles from the city on the
road to Gabii. The trauma produced by the Gallic sack was consider-
able: Livy's history repeatedly tells of the Romans levying and mobiliz-
ing armies in response to even the report of a Gallic uprising.

This passage is a good example of the way in which Livy uses descriptive details to convey national character. Here they set up a sharp
contrast between the flashy but insubstantial Gaul and the plainer but
steadfast Roman. Moreover, we have what was probably Livy's source

for this story, the version of the Roman annalist Claudius Quadrigarius. Comparing the two shows how Livy's many changes in detail produce a very different cumulative result. Quadrigarius' account can be found in H. Peter's *Historicorum Romanorum reliquae* (vol. i., Quadr. fr. 10), as well as in Oakley's *A Commentary on Livy VI–X* (vol. 2, pp. 113–114).

1   **dictator** Titus Quinctius Poenus, introduced at 6.42.4, where Livy says that he was made dictator in response to *fama repens Gallici belli* ("the sudden rumor of a war with Gaul")

tumultus Gallici gen.; *tumultus* can refer either to a sudden outbreak of violence or the emergency measures taken in response to one.

2   **sacramento adegit** "he bound by an oath"

3   **citeriore ripa Anienis** the river Anio, modern Aniene. The bridge was on the Via Salaria, the old road that led from the salt beds at the Tiber mouth inland into the Apennines. It left Rome by the Colline Gate.

4   **rumpentibus** sc. *pontem*

7   **eximia corporis magnitudine** descriptive abl. The extraordinary size of the opponent is a frequent topos in descriptions of single combat.

8   **quem** antecedent is *uirum* from line 9

10   **noster duorum euentus** lit. "both our outcomes," which means "our relative success"

12–13 **cum . . . uererentur et . . . nollent** circumstantial *cum*-clauses

T. Manlius L. Filius The patronymic adds dignity; it also helps to recall a story of this Manlius and his father told by Livy at 7.4–5. The senior Manlius had treated his son harshly, but in spite of that his son defended him from the legal attack of a tribune.

14   **ex statione** Manlius leaves his position. Note Livy's uses of *statio* at 27 and 46 as well. The three references to Manlius', as well as the Roman soldiers', keeping or leaving their positions, convey a sense of order and discipline.

15   **ad dictatorem pergit** We might expect Manlius to head
      straight for the Gaul; it comes as a slight surprise that he
      leaves his position only to make his way to the dictator.

      'iniussu tuo' inquit . . . This conversation makes Manlius an
      example of deference to authority; moreover it allows him to
      recall both a family exploit and his habit of respectful conduct
      towards his father.

16   **pugnauerim** potential subjunctive referring to the future

19   **'quae Gallorum agmen ex rupe Tarpeia deiecit'** During the
      siege of 390 BCE, M. Manlius saved the citadel from a night
      attack. He was rewarded with the cognomen *Capitolinus*. T.
      Manlius does not elaborate on this accomplishment, which
      Livy relates at Book 5.47, possibly because M. Manlius Capi-
      tolinus was later executed for inciting sedition (Book 6.20).

20–21 **'macte uirtute . . . ac pietate . . . esto'** "be blessed for your
      courage and sense of duty."

21–23 **nomen . . . praesta** *praestare*, with a predicate adj. means "to
      render" or "to keep." The consul's formal granting of permis-
      sion makes Manlius the representative of his people.

      pedestre scutum "a foot-soldier's shield"

      Hispano . . . gladio . . . habili The Spanish sword was short,
      and suitable for thrusting, whereas the Gallic sword was lon-
      ger, more easily bent, and more suitable for slashing.

24   **armatum adornatumque** an amplifying pair of alliterative adjs.

25–26 **quoniam id quoque memoria dignum antiquis uisum est**
      Livy's description of the Gaul's behavior is also a comment on
      the cruder taste of earlier historians.

      linguam . . . exserentem part of a display meant to intimidate
      the opponent.

27   **recipiunt inde se ad stationem** Livy again draws attention to
      the soldiers' return to this position, in order to convey the near-
      ceremonial nature of the preparations.

28   **spectaculi magis more quam lege belli** "more in the manner
      of an exhibition than according to the law of war"

29 **uisu ac specie** abl. of specification

aestimantibus dat. of person judging

alteri possessive dat.

30–31 **uersicolori ... armis** This emphasis on color and superficial decoration sets up the opposition between appearance and substance which is characteristic of Livy's treatment of, and the Roman attitude in general towards, the Gauls.

32 **in armis habilibus magis quam decoris** "wearing arms more useful than handsome"

33–34 **uana / plenum** another opposition between Roman and Gaul

36–37 **tot ... pendentibus** abl. absolute

38 **caesim** adv. "with a slashing motion"

39 **ensem** only here in Livy, a poetic word

mucrone subrecto "with the blade of his sword in a vertical position"

40 **scuto scutum** The repetition of the same word in a different case is called polyptoton. It appears frequently in epic battle scenes, where the juxtaposition of the words reflects the clash of weapons.

interior with abl. "closer in (than)"

42 **uentrem atque inguina hausit** "he gouged his belly and groin so as to drain the blood," a poetic expression

43 **in spatium ingens ruentem** "collapsing so as to cover a great distance"

44 **corpus ab omni alia uexatione intactum** an important departure from the version of Quadrigarius, in which Manlius cuts off the Gaul's head.

uno torque abl. of separation, with *spoliauit*; the torque, a collar of twisted metal, was the characteristic military ornament of a Gaul (cf. Vergil *Aen.* 8.660–61 on the Gauls attacking the Capitoline: *tum lactea colla / auro innectuntur*, "moreover their milk-white necks are bound with gold").

45–48 **defixerat ... Gallos: Romani ... perducunt** an elegant chiasmus

48–49   **carminum prope in modum** "almost in the manner of songs"

Torquati cognomen a limiting gen. instead of a noun in apposition. As he did in the case of Mucius Scaevola, here too Livy concludes an episode with the explanation of a cognomen.

50   **familiae honori** take *familiae* and *honori* as double dat.

51–52   **dictator** By closing with the dictator's praise, the episode reinforces the importance of his authority. A crucial feature of Manlius' achievement is that he played according to the rules. This same T. Manlius orders his own son executed for engaging in single combat without permission (Book 8.7–8). In 216 BCE another severe Manlius Torquatus argues against ransoming the Romans taken prisoner at Cannae.

coronam auream . . . donum Golden crowns are rewarded to individual soldiers elsewhere in Book 7: to Manlius here, to Marcus Valerius Corvus in 7.26, and to Publius Decius in 7.37. Livy represents Marcius Valerius as consciously emulating Manlius' achievement.

mirisque . . . laudibus tulit "he praised to an amazing degree"

◌ *From the third decade* (*Books 21–30*)
The causes of the Second Punic War, 21.1.1–2.2

Books 11–20 of Livy's history are lost. They included accounts of Rome's war with Pyrrhus of Epirus and the First Punic War. Books 21–30 are devoted largely to the Second Punic War, with the First Macedonian War brought in as it impinges on or detracts from Rome's efforts in the war against Carthage. In its careful arrangement and focus on Rome's struggle with Carthage, Livy's third decade calls to mind the contemporary *Aeneid*. In this passage, Livy introduces his topic, asserts the magnitude of his theme, and gives the causes of the conflict.

1–2   **in parte operis mei** *in parte* is emphatic; the entire phrase forms a contrast with *in principio summae totius*. Livy asserts the magnitude of both his immediate topic, the war, and his project of writing Rome's history *ab urbe condita*.

licet mihi praefari In contrast to *professi . . . sunt*, the impers. *licet* suggests the legitimacy of Livy's claim as opposed to those of *plerique . . . rerum scriptores*, "most historians."

praefari "to say by way of preface," an expression that recalls Livy's preface to his entire work

quod . . . = [sc. *id*] *quod*, which looks ahead to the indirect statement in 2–4: *bellum . . . me scripturum*

summae totius *summa* here = "the whole of a thing as distinct from the parts composing it" (*OLD* s.v. *summa*, 5)

rerum scriptores "historians." *Res*, or *res gestae*, can mean both historical events and the record of events.

2–4 **bellum . . . memorabile . . . me scripturum** indirect speech, introduced by *praefari*; Livy's educated readers would surely think of Herodotus 7.20–21, on the size of Xerxes' expedition against Greece, and Thucydides 1.1–21, on the magnitude and importance of the Peloponnesian War.

omnium [sc. bellorum] antecedent of *quae*

gesta sint subjunctive in a subordinate clause in indirect speech. *Bellum gerere* is the Latin idiom for to "wage war," but in the context discussing memory and historians, *rerum scriptores*, the verb *gerere* in *gesta sint* also takes on its connotations of achievement (e.g., *res gestae*).

4–5 **quod . . . gessere** (*gessere = gesserunt*) the construction is *bellum . . . quod . . . Carthaginiensis . . . gesserunt*; simple rel., not part of the indirect statement with *bellum* as antecedent of *quod*

Hannibale duce In emphatic position, the abl. absolute distinguishes this Punic War from the other two.

Carthaginienses cum populo Romano Livy focuses on the two peoples; no one Roman counterpart appears as a match for Hannibal. Moreover, in a work that sets down the *res gestae* of the Roman people, it is striking that the Carthaginians are the subject of the verb *gerere*. Indeed Book 21 begins with events in Carthage, and turns to Rome only when the people of Saguntum, in Spain, besieged by Hannibal's men, send envoys to the Senate to ask for help. Thus both the syntax of the opening sentence and the spatial organization of the book underscore the fact that the Carthaginians were the aggressors.

5–10 **Nam . . . qui uicerunt** This sentence explains why the war was the most memorable, and thus why Livy is permitted to make his claim. It accumulates reasons without being repetitive. Note first *neque . . . neque*; then *et . . . et*; and finally *etiam . . . etiam*. Note also the doubling of nouns and adjs., some antithetical, others nearly redundant, for the sake of expansion: *ciuitates gentesque . . . uirium aut roboris . . . haud ignotas . . . sed expertas . . . uaria fortuna . . . ancepsque Mars.*

opibus abl. of specification; for the pl. see *OLD* s.v. *ops*, 3: "the means one has at one's disposal for a purpose," "resources" (military, economic, etc.)

6 **contulerunt arma** *conferre arma* is "to direct or aim weapons"

his ipsis dat. of possession

7 **uirium aut roboris** partitive gens. after *tantum*; Greenough points out the nice distinction in meaning between *uires*, active strength and fighting power, and *robur*, pass. strength, with an almost moral dimension, i.e., the stuff of which the soldiers were made.

7–8 **haud ignotas belli artes inter sese sed expertas** *ignotas* and *expertas* are predicate adjs.; the force of *inter se* falls on them equally.

8–9 **primo Punico . . . bello** abl. of time when; the First Punic War, 264–241 BCE.

sese = se

conserebant The object is *artes*, the construction an extension of the usual *conserere manum / dextras / proelium / certamen*. The impf. conveys the ongoing nature of the struggle: this was not limited to the beginning of the conflict.

Mars warfare personified

10 **fuerint** not the expected impf. subjunctive, but the pf., to show that this is historical fact.

propius compar. of the prep. *prope*, which takes the acc.

10–14 **Odiis etiam . . . Fama est etiam** Livy introduces the last two reasons with *etiam . . . etiam*: "moreover . . . and furthermore . . . " Having dealt with resources and fighting strength, he now turns to emotions. The sentence structure is typical of historical narrative: a main clause, then expansion by means of the abl. absolute.

Odiis with *maioribus*; *odiis* is in the emphatic first position.

prope softens the claim somewhat

12–13 **quod . . . inferrent arma** the clause with the subjunctive expresses the reason for the Romans' resentment

Poenis sc. *indignantibus*, a second abl. absolute

quod . . . crederent the reason for the Carthaginians' resentment

imperitatum impers. with *esse*; takes the dat.

13–14 **Fama est** Livy often introduces anecdotes with some such expression. Polybius tells a version of this story at 3.11.1–7; Cornelius Nepos at *Hannibal* 2.3–6. Both Polybius and Nepos put the story in the mouth of Hannibal himself.

Hannibalem . . . blandientem . . . admotum . . . adactum The pples. modifying *Hannibalem* tie the sentence together.

annorum with *nouem*: in 237 BCE

15 **blandientem** + dat. "cajoling," "begging"

16 **eo** to Spain

17–18 **iure iurando** "by an oath," usually treated as one word, *iusiurandum*

se . . . hostem fore populo Romano the substance of the oath

cum primum posset "as soon as he could"

fore = *futurum esse*

hostem + dat.

Angebant in the emphatic first position. Its position, next to *ingentis*, a word denoting expansiveness, makes it even more striking.

19   **ingentis spiritus** descriptive gen.

          Sicilia Sardiniaque amissae the pple. with substantive force,
          "the loss of Sicily and Sardinia," another example of the *ab
          urbe condita* construction

19–22   **nam ... interceptam** indirect speech, giving Hamilcar's spe-
          cific painful thoughts about the loss of Sicily and Sardina

          nimis celeri desperatione rerum Hamilcar felt that the Car-
          thaginian defeat was not thorough enough to justify giving up
          claims to Sicily.

          Sardiniam ... interceptam The Romans took possession of
          the island by exploiting a revolt of the Sardinians.

          inter motum Africae *motus* here refers to the revolt of Car-
          thage's unpaid mercenaries and Libyan subjects.

23   **sub recentem Romanam pacem** "right after the conclusion of
          peace with Rome."

          per quinque annos Livy is being schematic with his numbers.
          According to Polybius, 1.88, the war lasted three years and
          four months (late 241–early 237 BCE).

25   **augendo Punico imperio** abl. of manner with *se ... gessit*; in
          later writers this is almost equivalent to a pres. pple.

26–27   **si diutius uixisset ... inlaturos fuisse** Past contrafactual con-
          dition in indirect speech.

Hannibal crosses the Alps, 21.35.4–12

After capturing Saguntum, Hannibal marches westward, avoiding
contact with the Romans as much as possible. He turns inland at the
Rhone delta, and makes for the Alps. It is a bold move, because of the
difficult nature of the mountain passes and the uncertain loyalty of
the mountain-dwellers, who at one point ambush the Carthaginian
column and separate the soldiers from their baggage. The elephants
are both an aid and a hindrance: their strange appearance scares the
locals, but their size makes it difficult for them to make their way
along the narrow mountain paths.

1   **Nono die** This detail emphasizes the difficulty of reaching the pass, especially with so many pack animals in need of fodder.

    iugum "the pass"

    peruentum est impers.

    inuia pleraque substantive, "many pathless places" or "mostly pathless places"

2   **iis** refers to *ducentium*. This is analogous to the expression *fides habere* (+ dat.), "to place trust in": "when there was no trust in them [*iis*]."

3   **a coniectantibus iter** *iter* is the direct object of *coniectatibus*, which is an abl. of agent with *initae*

4   **statiua** n. pl. as substantive, "a rest period during a march"

    habita [sc. sunt]

    fessis an example of hyperbaton. The position of *fessis* far from *militibus* gives it emphasis.

5   **aliquot** indecl.

6   **sequendo** the gerund with direct object *uestigia*

    peruenere = peruenerunt

7   **Fessis** The repetition of this word, again in the initial position, emphasizes the exhaustion of both man and beast.

    taedio with gen.

    niuis etiam casus The fall of snow exacerbates an already harsh situation.

7–8   **occidente iam sidere Vergiliarum** The setting of this constellation, the Pleides, means that it is late October by the modern calendar.

11–12 **praegressus** transitive here

    in . . . quodam Construe with *consistere iussis militibus*.

13   **Alpinis montibus** dat. after *subiectos*

14   **moeniaque . . .** Livy moves into implied indirect speech as Hannibal moves from pointing out the features of the landscape to showing his men how easy the conquest of Italy will be.

14–15   **moeniaque . . . Italiae** also Cato the Elder's image (Servius
        ad *Aen.* 10.13: *Alpes quae secundum Catonem et Liuium muri
        uice tuebantur Italiam,* "the Alps, which, according to Cato
        and Livy, protected Rome as walls")

15–16   **plana, procliuia** *plana* = "simple" or "straightforward," as
        well as "level"; *procliua* = "requiring no effort" or "easy," as
        well as "sloping downward." Hannibal combines topographi-
        cal description with metaphorical language: the lay of the
        land from the Alps to Rome is not always literally "level" and
        "sloping downward," because the Appenines are in the way.

        summum adv. "at most"

16–17   **arcem et caput Italiae** i.e., Rome; cf. 1.55.6, on the human
        head discovered during the digging for the temple of Jupiter
        on the Capitoline: *quae uisa species haud per ambages arcem
        eam imperii caputque rerum fore portendebat.*

18   **nihil** direct object of *temptantibus*

20–21   **sicut** the correlative (with *ita*), with concessive force

        pleraque Alpium "most [places] of the Alps"

        ab Italia "on the Italian side"

22–25   **praeceps, angusta, lubrica** This accumulation of adjs. is a
        means of rhetorical amplification.

        ut . . . possent . . . -que occiderent result clauses

        qui paulum titubassent a conditional rel. clause

        uestigio suo dat., with *haerere*

Scipio addresses his army, 21.40.6–11

At this point the two armies are nearly in sight of each other. The Roman commander, having led his troops across the Po and taken up
a position on the river Ticinus, addresses his troops. This is Publius
Cornelius Scipio, consul in 218 BCE, and father of the great Publius
Cornelius Scipio who will defeat Hannibal and acquire the cognomen *Africanus.* Livy balances these two speeches, which mark the

first meeting of the Romans and Carthaginians, with a pair in Book 30, delivered by Hannibal and (the future) Africanus before the decisive Roman victory at Zama.

Scipio addresses an army that is both inexperienced and new to him. One of his rhetorical goals, then, is to increase his listeners' confidence. In the first part of the speech, Scipio does so by insisting that everything is under control, that the Roman senate and people have chosen him, a consul, to lead the fighting against Hannibal, and that, moreover, he has chosen to serve with these men in Italy rather than with his veterans in Spain. In the excerpt included here he reminds his men that Rome has beaten Carthage before, that Hannibal's men fight out of necessity rather than daring, and that, furthermore, they are worn out from crossing the Alps.

Scipio's speech achieves liveliness and vigor in several ways: one is the generally striking images of wasted men and exhausted animals; another is asyndeton, the avoidance of conjunctions, especially from *effigies* in line 9 to *habetis* in line 14; a third is the figure called *congeries*, the heaping up of nouns and adjectives.

2   **uobis illisque . . . uictoribus . . . uictis** poss. dats.

4   **perierint . . . supersint** subjunctive in causal rel. clauses

5   **qui . . . detractauere** The rel. precedes its antecedent, *eos*.

7   **At enim** Scipio anticipates a potential objection to his argument.

   quidem concessive here, "admittedly"

8–9 **quorum . . . possit** rel. clause expressing result

   robora ac uires the ideas of defensive and offensive strength mentioned in the preface to Book 21

   Effigies used metaphorically here: "spectres" or "ghosts"

   immo this particle introduces a correction of a previous statement

11–13 **ad hoc . . . equi** N.B. how Livy varies the word order and connectives in this list: he achieves amplification without boring repetition.

13   **cum hoc . . . cum hoc** the rhetorical figure anaphora

16–20   **Sed ita forsitan decuit . . . deos ipsos . . . committere ac prof-
          ligare bellum, nos . . . conficere** Adversative asyndeton; *deos
          ipsos* and *nos* serves in place of a conj. Translate "but."

          cum + abl. of accompaniment (*cum . . . ruptore . . . committere
          . . . bellum*)

          secundum prep. + acc.

Scipio concludes his speech, 21.41.13–17

According to Scipio, a number of other factors besides the Carthaginians' exhaustion should install confidence: his decision to lead this
army instead of the one in Spain; his previous defeat of the Carthaginians in a cavalry skirmish near the Rhone; the Roman victory over
Carthage in the First Punic War. Scipio concludes by pointing out
that, glory aside, his army has no choice but to defend Italy.

1–2   **utinam . . . esset** optative subjunctive "would that there were"
          tantum "only"

2–3   **de posessione Siciliae ac Sardiniae** *de* + abl., to fight for
          something as for a prize; in Sicily and Sardinia, cf. 21.1.2.

4   **ab tergo** "at our back"

6   **quas . . . possint** rel. clause of characteristic

7   **ante Romana moenia** This image reinforces the sense of crisis.

8–13   **Vnusquisque . . .** Scipio's closing words aim to make each sol-
          dier's view of his own responsibility expand from protecting
          his own body to embracing his immediate family, and then
          including the entire Roman world, both city and empire.

10   **reputet** The third in a series of jussive subjunctives (after
          putet and *agitet*), *reputet* introduces the indirect statements
          intueri . . . senatum populumque Romanum and *talem . . .
          fortunam . . . fore.*

11–13   **qualis . . . fuerit, talem . . . fore** *fuerit* is pf. subjunctive; "as
          . . . was [on this specific occasion] . . . so . . . shall be"

Hannibal illustrates the nature of the situation, 21.42–43.10

After Scipio's speech, Livy shifts attention abruptly to Hannibal, who must put heart into an army that is worn out from crossing the Alps. Hannibal does so first by presenting them with a spectacle that makes clear the dire nature of their situation, then by rousing them with words.

One effect of Livy's placing this account of single combat between the two speeches is to make a sharp contrast between Scipio's words and Hannibal's illustration. It is instructive to compare his sequence of speeches and events with those of Polybius at 3.62–64. Polybius presents Hannibal's spectacle and speech first, then turns to Scipio. His versions of both speeches are shorter and summarize much of what each man says instead of quoting it.

1–2   **Haec apud Romanos consul** [sc. *dixit*], a trenchant and almost epic transition. The word order sets Scipio and Hannibal against one another.

1–5   A good example of the use of pples. to expand a sentence: *Hannibal . . . ratus, circumdato . . . exercitu captiuos . . . uinctos . . . statuit armisque . . . proiectis . . . iussit.*

      rebus prius quam uerbis Hannibal's putting deeds before words anticipates the effectiveness of his strategy.

      adhortandos [sc. *esse*]

      ad spectaculum The reference to spectacle is repeated below in 12, *spectantes*. Livy offers this sight to readers for their education as well: Hannibal's men receive a vivid image of their situation; the reader receives a vivid image of the great general's leadership.

      armisque Gallicis . . . interpretem These details show how, although the Gauls differ from the Carthaginians in customs, language, and arms, they share the desire to fight for prizes and glory.

5–6   **ecquis . . . uellet** indir. question after *interrogare*, serving as the apodosis of a fut. more vivid condition with the protasis *si . . . leuaretur . . . et . . . acciperet*. See Bennett 301, 319.

ad unum "as one"

7   **in id** "for this purpose"

8   **\<ut\>** not in the main manuscripts

9–10   **cuiusque sors exciderat, alacer** [sc. *is*]: *is cuiusque sors exciderat, alacer . . .*

alacer, inter gratulantes gaudio exsultans The several words denoting mental states and their expression together reinforce the idea that each man chosen by lot represents the attitude of all.

10–12   **ubi . . . dimicarent** an iterative subjunctive in a past general condition

is habitus animorum "this cast of spirits"

non . . . modo . . . sed etiam "not only . . . but also"

inter with *homines*

13   **bene morientium** not just dying, but dying *well*

fortuna Like Scipio's speech, this scene closes with a reference to *fortuna*; Hannibal's speech will open with one.

Having presented the grisly spectacle of single combat between prisoners, Hannibal interprets it for his men. His discussion of their situation and their fortune brings together the ideas of necessity and reward that served as motivating forces in historiography as early as Herodotus. Having crossed the Alps, the Carthaginians are in no condition to retreat back over them. Constrained by mountain and river, they have no choice but to fight, and to move forward in the only direction they can, towards Rome, where rich spoils await them.

14   **adfectos** Hannibal's soldiers are "strongly moved" or "affected."

15   **ita . . . locutus fertur** "[Hannibal] is said to have spoken thus." Livy introduced Scipio's speech with the words *talem orationem est exorsus*, "he began a speech of this kind" (21.39.10). In neither case can Livy have had access to the words actually spoken; rather, he follows the regular historiographical

practice of writing down words that suited both the characters who speak them and the situations in which they speak.

16–17   **in alienae sortis exemplo** the word order forms a chiastic structure with *in aestimanda fortuna uestra*. The contrast emphasized is between *exemplo* and *aestimanda*, as well as between *alienae sortis* and *fortuna uestra*. The Carthaginian soldiers must calculate (*aestimare*) the nature of their situation from the paradigm (*exemplum*) of another that they have seen.

18   **uicimus** "we have [already] conquered," the pf. indicative instead of *uincemus* in a fut. more vivid condition

19   **quaedam ueluti imago** "a certain reflection, as it were"; the inclusion of *ueluti* shows that Hannibal is using the word as a metaphor. Livy also uses *imago*, without *ueluti*, with the meaning of "model," or "example," e.g., *cladis imaginem Furculas Caudinas memorabant*, "they recalled the Caudine Forks as an example of disaster."

20   **nescio an** "I dare say"

       uincula the metaphorical chains recall the real ones that bound the Gallic captives

22–24   **claudunt . . . urgent** verbs conveying the idea of constriction and pressure. The landscape here is active: the seas close in on the Carthaginians; the Po and the Alps press upon them. Recall that when Hannibal was trying to encourage his men in the Alps, he pointed out that Italy sloped easily downwards to Rome. He adapts his presentation of Italy's geography to his immediate rhetorical goals.

23   **circa** adv. "round about" Does this reflect the actual geography, in that the Carthaginians are in either a bend of a river or between the Po and its tributary, or is this another case of Livy's Hannibal adapting geography to make a point?

       Padus amnis, maior [Padus] the editors (for this section, Conway and Walters) would delete the second *Padus*. It is in the main manuscripts, and possibly was repeated for rhetorical effect.

25-26   **Hic uicendum aut moriendum est** Hannibal's words recall
        the description of his spectacle: *ut non uincentium magis*
        quam bene morientium fortuna laudaretur.

25-41   **et eadem fortuna** Hannibal's emphasis shifts from necessity to
        prizes: *praemia . . . ampliora; ampla pretia; opimam mercedem;*
        opulenta . . . ditia stipendia; magna . . . pretia; dignam mercedem

36-37   **pecora consectando nullum emolumentum . . . uidistis** the
        OLD notes that *emolumentum*, from *emolo*, "to produce by
        grinding out," probably originally meant "output from a mill."
        Thus Hannibal's words include a subtle contrast between the
        nomadic life of the herdsman following flocks in the desolate
        wastes of Lusitania and Celtiberia and the settled life of the
        farmer in agrarian Italy.

40-41   **Hic . . . hic** the anaphora brings Hannibal's words to an emo-
        tional climax before he turns to his next point (not included
        here): that winning might not be as hard as his men expect

        emeritis stipendiis abl. with predicate adj. *dignam. Emerere*
        stipendium means to complete one's term in the army.

Hannibal concludes his speech, 21.44.1–9

In the intervening passage (21.43.11–18), Hannibal tells his men that
they should not consider winning to be difficult, because, having
spent the last twenty years campaigning, they are ready for this expedition; moreover, they have gained even more experience fighting their way to Italy through tribes of hostile Spaniards and Gauls.
Most important of all, whereas Scipio is leading a new and untried
army, Hannibal knows his men, and they know him. Experience has
taught him what they can do.

In this passage, Hannibal points out that, in addition to courage
and a fighting spirit, his men should have a sense of anger at the injustice done them by the settlements after the First Punic War.

1-5   **Quocumque . . . pugnaturos** a sentence typical of direct speech
        in Livy, in that it reaches syntactical completion at *roboris*, but

is then expanded. This a formal, yet also emotionally charged, sentence: it has interlocking word order of modifiers and nouns (*ueteranum peditem, generosissimarum gentium equites*), anaphora (*uos . . . uos*), correlatives: *cum . . . tum*, alliteration (*generosissimarum gentium . . . fidelissimos fortissimosque*), and four superlatives.

1   **circumtuli oculos** *circumfero* = "to turn" the eyes (or face, hands, etc.)

animorum "courage." The pl. reflects strong emotion.

2   **roboris** both physical strength and mental resolve

3   **frenatos infrenatosque** "bridled" and "unbridled." The second refers to the Numidians. Elsewhere in Livy *infrenare* also means "to bridle," e.g., at 37.20.5: *non stratos, non infrenatos magna pars habebant equos.*

5–8   **Inferimus . . . arcentis** another vigorous yet formal sentence, one that reaches syntactical completion early, with *descendiumus in Italiam*, and is then expanded by a participial phrase, *tanto . . . pugnaturi . . .*

infestisque signis an indication of attack, cf. Caesar, *BC* 7.51.3: *legiones . . . infestis contra hostis signis constiterunt*

7   **maior . . . maior** The anaphora and asyndeton add vehemence.

8–9   **inferentis uim** avoids repetition of *inferre bellum*

Accendit . . . et stimulat The verbs take on emphasis from their position at the beginning of each clause.

dolor, iniuria, indignitas Livy also uses asyndeton with the triple subject for emphasis

9–10   **Ad supplicium** in the emphatic initial position

11   **oppugnassetis** = *oppugnauissetis*

deditos a conditional use of the pple. ("*if* surrendered")

13   **sua** predicate adj.

suique arbitrarii predicate use of the gen.

15–16   **Circumscribit includitque** Once again, the verbs are at the front and emphatic.

terminis montium fluminumque Hannibal again raises the idea of being hemmed in by a place. (The Romans shut us in, with rivers and mountains so we had to leave; we are now shut in by a river [the Po] and by mountains [the Alps], so we have to fight our way out.)

17–22 **"Ne transieris Hiberum . . . "** Such imaginary dialogue is a figure of speech called *sermocinatio*. Hannibal's next words mirror the Romans' progressive transgression into the provinces of Carthage, even as the Romans themselves tell the Carthaginians not to stir from their position.

20 **<ademisti>** *ademisti? Adimis* is a conjecture (Heerwagen's) to give each of the sentences the verb it needs.

25–30 Hannibal repeatedly brings up the alternatives: victory, or death. Livy constructs the sentence around the antithesis: *illis/uobis*; *licet/necesse est*; *timidis et ignauis/fortibus uiris*. Yet within that structure he also achieves variation: rel. clauses describe the Romans' situation, an abl. absolute that of the Carthaginians.

25 **respectum** "a refuge." Both Scipio and Hannibal make it clear to their men that there is nowhere to retreat.

26 **sua terra, suus ager per tuta ac pacata itinera** the repetition of near-synonyms for the sake of amplificiation

30–31 **Si hoc . . . uicistis** With *iterum dicam*, Hannibal returns to his starting point.

[bene fixum] this appears in the main manuscripts, but probably entered the text as a gloss on *destinatum*

animo here, "mind" or "spirit"

31–32 **nullum contemptu m<ortis incitamentum>** Frigell's conjecture; the main manuscripts have *nullum contemptum*.

33 **acrius** with *incitamentum*; a good example of hyperbaton, Bennett 350, 11, a

The day after Cannae, 22.51.1–9

In Books 21 and 22, Livy tells how Rome suffered a series of progressively disastrous defeats at the hands of Hannibal and his army. The worst of these was at Cannae (modern Canne) in Apulia on the right bank of the river Aufidus. At this place, in August 216 BCE, Hannibal enveloped and annihilated two Roman consular armies, a body of fighting men possibly twice the size of his own, although the numbers are much debated.

Livy's account of the fighting itself is fairly perfunctory, except when he reports individual acts of heroism (e.g., an orderly offering a wounded consul his horse, the consul refusing). What interested Livy were the ways in which different people responded to Cannae: Hannibal, the wounded on the battlefield, the Roman survivors caught in their camp, and the Senate and people receiving the terrible news in Rome. In this passage, a wounded Numidian solder, dragged out from under the body of a dead Roman, bears marks that foreshadow the Romans' collective determination to defeat Carthage.

1   **Hannibali uictori** dat. with *gratularentur*

         ceteri in contrast to Maharbal (line 4)

2   **tanto . . . bello** abl. with *perfunctus*

2–3   **diei quod reliquum esset noctisque insequentis** *diei* depends on *quod*; *noctisque insequentis* on *quietem*. *Quod* is in apposition to *quietem*. His advisors urge Hannibal to give the men "as rest what remained of the day and the following night." (Compare 21.11.3 *paucorum iis dierum quietem dedit*, "he gave them a few days' rest.")

3–4   **sumeret . . . daret** depends on *suaderent ut*

4   **Maharbal** Hannibal's chief cavalry officer; he commanded the right wing at Cannae. Livy also mentions his role at Lake Trasimene.

         praefectus equitum *praefectus* + gen. = "officer in command of"

5 **cessandum** in an impers. gerundive construction *minime cessandum ratus*, "thinking that there should be no holding back."
The pf. pple. of *ratus* is regularly used in the sense of a pres. pple.

Immo particle used to introduce a correction of either the
preceding statement or an idea in it

Not only is Maharbal the subject of the sentence, but his trenchant and memorable statements are in direct speech, in contrast to Hannibal's response, which is not.

ut . . . scias a purpose clause

quid hac pugna sit actum indirect question introduced by *scias*

6 **uictor in Capitolio epulaberis** With the verb *epulaberis*, "you
will banquet," Livy's Maharbal makes a more extravagant
claim than Cato's (*die quinti in Capitolio tibi cena cocta erit*,
"on the fifth day dinner will be cooked for you on the Capitoline"), adapted by the historian Coelius (*die quinti Romae
in Capitolium curabo tibi cena sit cocta*). Hannibal will dine
in the presence of the three great Capitoline deities, Juppiter,
Juno, and Minerva, on the hill that was both the metaphorical
"head" of Rome (Livy 1.55) and the terminus of a victorious
general's triumphal procession.

7 **ut prius uenisse quam uenturum sciant** sc. *te*, "in order that
they [the Romans] learn of your arrival before your approach"

8–9 **maiorque . . . ut . . . posset** result clause

statim the important word here

10–11 **ad consilium pensandum . . . opus esse** This continues the
indirect statement, although Livy does not repeat the verb of
speaking.

ad consilium pensandum "for pondering strategy"

temporis a rare use of the gen. with *opus est*

eidem dat.

12 **dedere** = *dederunt*

13–14 **satis** adv. with *creditur*

saluti fuisse urbi atque imperio double dat. construction.

15   **foedamque** predicate adj. modifying *stragem*

16   **etiam hostibus** dat. of the person judging; *etiam* adds emphasis. The sight is terrible, even to the Carthaginians.

      insistunt with *ad* and the gerundive only here; *ad* governs both *spolia legenda* and *spectandam stragem*. The rest of the passage is an extraordinarily vivid description of the dead and dying. By pointing out that the victors went out to look upon the carnage, and that it was a terrible sight even for enemy, Livy makes readers see the battlefield through the Carthaginians' eyes.

      Iacebant The verb is at the beginning for emphasis.

17–18 **ut quem cuique fors aut pugna iunxerat aut fuga** The haphazard situation of the dead and wounded is in contrast to the ordered categories in the description that follows, which shows a progression in Roman willingness to die.

      ut here, the rel. adv.

      quem cuique *-que* is doing double duty; translate as if *quemque cuique*

18–23 **adsurgentes quidam . . . quosdam et iacentes uiuos . . . inuenti quidam sunt . . .** The repetition of *quidam* keeps attention focused on the categories of dying and dead; yet Livy avoids monotony by varying its position and case.

19   **ex strage media** "from the midst of the carnage"

19–20 **stricta . . . uolnera** "wounds that had been drawn together," that is, staunched by the cold, thus reviving the afflicted.

23   **mersis . . . capitibus** abl. absolute, "their heads thrust." The downward motion of *mersis* is opposed to *adsurgentes* (line 18).

24–25 **quos . . . fecisse foueas . . . interclusisse spiritum** indirect statement depending on *apparebat*

      quos sibi ipsos Note that the pers. prons. are, as is usual, clustered together.

      superiecta humo abl. of means with *obruentes*

25   **praecipue conuertit** placed at the beginning for emphasis

      conuertit sc. *in se*

26–27 **subtractus Numida mortuo superincubanti Romano uiuus**
The interlocking word order juxtaposes the living and the
dead; *Numida mortuo . . . Romano uiuus. Superincubare*, "to
lie on top," appears only here.

naso auribusque lacertis abl. absolute

27–29 **cum . . . exspirasset** sc. *Romanus*

manibus . . . inutilibus abl. absolute

in rabiem ira uersa abl. absolute

laniando dentibus hostem Livy here uses the abl. of the ger-
und to express manner. It is nearly the equivalent of a pres.
pple.: "tearing the enemy with his teeth." This use of the ger-
und is more common in late and medieval Latin.

᭪ *From the fourth decade* (*Books 31–40*)
The Bacchic "conspiracy"

Bacchus is identified with Dionysus, son of Zeus and Semele, who
was taken from his mother's womb as she lay dying and was reborn
from Zeus' thigh. Bacchus is traditionally both the inventor of wine
and the god of wine and intoxication. His other spheres of influence
are the theater, ritual madness (distinct from intoxication), and the
afterlife. In Greece the worshippers who entered into the state of ritual ecstasy were generally women; yet festivals in honor of Dionysius
also included cross-dressing on the part of men and, at Athens, pa-
rades of processions bearing *phalloi*. A transgressive god, with both
masculine and feminine traits, Bacchus challenged neat conceptual
categories, and his cult could threaten social order. Greek accounts,
such as the one in Euripides' *Bacchae*, assign him a foreign origin,
in Asia Minor, and preserve a tradition of resistance to his worship.
At Rome he became identified with the Italian god of fertility, Liber
Pater, whose name, like Bacchus, is a metonym for wine.

The harsh suppression of the cult at Rome in 186 BCE, and the
strictures placed on other "exotic" cults such as that of the Magna
Mater (brought to Rome from Asia Minor in 205 BCE), demonstrate
an increasing wariness on Rome's part towards foreign religions

during the late third and early second centuries. Livy's account of the scandal of the Bacchanalia, however, probably reflects Augustan attitudes towards religion more than the reality of the original events. For example, he presents the cult as a pernicious novelty, but casual remarks about Bacchus in Plautus' plays (presented ca. 205–184 BCE) show that the god was fairly familiar to Roman audiences by this time. Livy's account should be read for what it is: a lively social drama, whose focus on sympathetic individual characters lends a sense of urgency to the actions of the consul and senate.

The beginning of the Bacchic conspiracy, 39.9.1–7

Livy introduces the matter of the Bacchanalia at 39.8.1, presenting it as a distraction from the consuls' traditional military duties abroad: "The following year saw the consuls Sp. Postumius Albinus and Q. Marcius Philippus averted from military command and provincial administration to the suppression of a domestic conspiracy." Before beginning his account of this "conspiracy," Livy notes that the cult of Bacchus was brought to Etruria by a Greek; he then describes the morally corrupt practices of the devotees of Bacchus, which included nocturnal meetings of members of both sexes, excessive feasting and drinking, and all manner of debauchery. The cult of Bacchus comes to the attention of the Roman officials because of the relationship between a young man of good family and his lover. The youth is P. Aebutius, whose father is dead, and whose stepfather has abused his role as guardian. Aebutius' lover is an ex-slave and prostitute, Hispala Faecina, who was introduced to the rites of Bacchus by her former mistress. Hispala is more generous to and protective of Aebutius than are his own mother and stepfather, who provide for him stingily and want to corrupt him by involving him in the cult of Bacchus.

1   **labes** "disaster" or "debacle," but the first meaning of the word is a "fall or subsidence of earth." It is related to the verbs *labo* and *labor*, which Livy uses in his metaphors for moral collapse in the preface to his work (*Praef.* 9: *labente deinde paulatim disciplina . . . deinde ut magis magisque lapsi sint . . .*).

1-2   **ex Etruria Romam . . . penetrauit** The phrase calls to mind the more pristine Rome of the first book, which saw the arrival in Rome of dangerous elements from Etruria, the Tarquins with their powerful women.

     contagione morbi abl. of means, "by the infection of a disease," another metaphor that recalls the preface, with its images of illness and health

2   **magnitudo urbis** yet another theme from the preface, where Livy points out that Rome struggles with its own magnitude

     capacior "more capable of holding," parallel with *patentior*, with the objective gen. *talium malorum*

3-4   **hoc maxime modo** "in this way for the most part." The phrase looks ahead to the story that follows.

     Postumium Sp. Postumius Albinus, together with Q. Marcius Philippus, consul for 186 BCE

     P. Aebutius The Aebutii were an old Roman *gens*. (Livy 3.6.1 records an Aebutius as consul.) The name was still around in Cicero's time.

5   **publico equo** *publicus* here means "maintained or provided by the state"

     pupillus a technical term for a minor under the care of a guardian

6   **tutela** the guardianship of a minor or other person not legally qualified to handle his/her affairs

8   **rationem reddere** "to render an account." Aebutius' stepfather has probably spent the money.

9   **obnoxium** + dat. "at the mercy of"

11-15   **se pro aegro eo uouisse . . . deducturam** indirect statement introduced by *appellat*; *ubi . . . uelle* is the substance of the vow.

12   **Bacchis** dat. with *initiaturam* "to consecrate"

     damnatam with gen. *uoti*, "obliged to fulfil the vow"

13   **decem dierum** "for a period of ten days"

14   **pure** "with ritual purity"

15   **deducturam** here the verb means "to escort" or "to accompany"

       Scortum nobile *nobile* here in the sense of "known"

15-16 **Hispala Faecenia** there is a town in Spain (site of the modern Seville) called Hispalis. The name, then, suggests Spanish origin.

16   **ancillula** "slave girl," a diminutive of *ancilla*, "female slave," itself a diminutive of *ancula*, "maidservant"

17   **eodem . . . genere** abl. of means

       Huic Hispala

18   **consuetudo** "intimacy"

       iuxta with acc. "in conformity with"

20-21 **maligne omnia praebentibus suis** "his own [relatives] providing all things meanly"

       meretriculae munificentia The idea of a "prostitute's bounty" contrasts sharply with the stinginess of Aebutius' relatives.

22   **patroni** Hispala's *patronus* is her former owner, who would inherit her property if she died childless or intestate.

       in nullius manu After the death of her *patronus*, Hispala had no legal guardian; but as a woman, even though she was in no one's *manus*, she was unable to make a will without obtaining a *tutor*, a guardian.

23-24 **testamentum . . . heredem** The Romans were highly interested in wills as vehicles for the transfer of property; making a will was a duty, *officium*. That Hispala takes this trouble and makes Aebutius her sole heir illustrates her generosity and the disinterested nature of her affection for him.

The Bacchic conspiracy (continued), 39.10.1–8

After providing the background of the characters involved and describing Aebutius' precarious situation, Livy focuses on the specific event that triggers the inquiry into the cult of Bacchus: Aebutius' telling Hispala that he needs to observe a period of sexual abstinence in order to be initiated into the cult. Hispala is shocked to learn that his own guardians wish him initiated. Her horrified response to the news alludes in general terms to the moral and physical corruption suffered by the cult's youthful initiates.

1　**Haec amoris pignora** the fact that Hispala made Aebutius her sole heir

1–2　**cum essent ... nec ... haberent** *cum* governs both subjunctives.

　　alter ab altero literally, "the one from the other," but better translated here as "from each other," since *alter* is used in a collective sense with the pl. verb.

　　per iocum indicates a circumstance attending the verb (here *uetat*)

3　**per aliquot noctes** *per* here means "over a period of"

3–4　**religionis se causa ... Bacchis initiari uelle** indirect speech, introduced by the idea of speaking implicit in *uetat*

5　**'Di meliora'** [sc. *faciant*] This is a colloquial expression, with about the emotional force of "god forbid!" or "good god!"

5–6　**mori ... quam id faceret** With *mori* we return to indirect speech.

7–9　**detestari** "to call down" (with *in* + acc.)

　　cum ... tum "both ... and"

　　exsecrationibus the act of cursing, cf. 8.7.21: *ut neque lamentis neque exsecrationibus parceretur*

　　matrem ... Once again we see indirect speech introduced by the idea of speaking in another verb, here *iubet*.

10　**'Vitricus ergo'** These and the following words are Hispala's.

10-11   **matrem . . . sit** Hispala tactfully separates Aebutius' stepfather and his mother.

      pudicitiam famam spem uitamque The heaping up (*congeries*) of nouns without a conj. (until *-que*) gives the effect off speed and violent emotion.

12   **perditum ire . . . properat** "he hastens to destroy"

      mirabundo "wondering" or "astonished at." The suffix *-bundus* produces verbal adjs. with an active force, some even taking a direct object.

13   **quid rei esset** indirect question after *quaeranti*

      precata "having invoked"

15-16   **ancillam . . . liberam** The antithesis takes the place of a coordinating conj. "but." From *ancillam* through *facienda essent* (lines 24–25) is Hispala's indirect statement.

16   **eo** to that place

      scire [sc. *se*]

17   **officinam** "a workshop"

      et iam biennio "and, now, for the past two years"

      constare "to be established"

18   **annis** abl. of comparison

18-22   **introductus sit . . . circumsonet . . . inferatur . . . possit** The tenses of the subjunctives show that Hispala's statement is in primary sequence, and that this part of her account (*ut quisque . . . possit*) should be translated in the pres.

      symphoniae "a band"

      ne . . . exaudiri possit a negative purpose clause, with a *cum* clause embedded within it

      Orare . . . obsecrare historical infinitives

23   **eo** correlative with *ubi* (line 24)

24   **infanda** modifies *omnia*, the subject of the clause

25   **fidem dedit** introduces the indirect statement *ab his sacris se temperaturum*

The magistrates learn of the conspiracy, 39.13.1–14

In 39.11–12, Livy reports that because of Hispala's warnings Aebutius refuses to be initiated into the cult. Angered at Aebutius' refusal, his mother and stepfather throw him out of their house. He then takes refuge with his aunt, Aebutia, who conveys his news of the conspiracy to Sulpicia, the mother-in-law of Sp. Postumius Albinus, one of the consuls. Sulpicia tells Postumius what Aebutia has told her.

In the passage included here, Postumius summons Hispala to an interview with him and Sulpicia. He first praises her for the information she has given and then, when she refuses to give more, grows angry and claims that Aebutius has already told him everything; she too had better tell all. His methods call to mind interrogation scenes in modern police drama, as does the intervention of Sulpicia, who plays "good cop" to his "bad."

1 **Mulier** i.e., Hispala

   haud dubie part of what Hispala, not the narrator, is thinking.

   id quod erat in apposition to *Aebutium indicem . . . esse*

2 **rata** pf. pple., normally translated as a pres., "thinking"

   Sulpiciae Sulpicia was introduced at 11.4 as a *gravis femina.*

3 **mulieris libertinae cum amatore sermonem** Livy portrays Hispala as invoking the conventional lightness of talk among lovers (cf. Catullus 10.5–6, trying to impress a friend's *scortilla*: *huc ut uenimus, incidere nobis / sermones uarii* "when we got here, there cropped up chit-chat on this topic and that").

4 **uerti** with in + acc., "to interpret as"

   rem . . . capitalem "a matter . . . punishable by death." Hispala responds here to the consul's vaguely worded threat that: "she would not receive the same mercy or goodwill should the information be exacted from her by another as she would if she confessed of her own accord," *non eandem . . . si coarguatur ab alio, ac per se fatenti veniam aut gratiam fore* (12.8).

5 **quo sciret quicquam** a relative clause of purpose

6-8   **hic . . . loqui** The consul draws a contrast between the lightness of lovers' talk and the dignity of the immediate surroundings.

6   **Hic** temporal, "at this point [in time]"

      tum quoque This is part of Postumius' statement, placed here for emphasis.

7   **cauillari** "to jest" or "banter"

8-9   **attolere . . . adhortarii . . . lenire** the historical infinitives convey the gradual and repetitive nature of Sulpicia's action

10   **incusata perfidia** abl. absolute

11-13 **magnum . . . maiorem multo** The parallel structure of the clauses here heightens the contrast between Hispala's fear of the gods and fear of men. That her fear of punishment at human hands is much greater than her fear of offending the gods may not say much for her *pietas*, but it helps to convey the enforced secrecy that made the Roman officials perceive the cult as a threat to social order.

13-14 **qui se indicem manibus suis discerpturi essent** This punishment calls to mind Pentheus' fate in Euripides' *Bacchae*.

      hoc . . . hoc Even when terrified, Hispala speaks with rhetorical flair.

16-17 **iubere . . . consul . . . dicere** more historical infinitives

18-26 From a respectable, three-day festival, limited to daylight and open to women only, the rites of Bacchus have expanded and become more inclusive.

21   **matronas** the word connotes respectability

22   **creari** with predicate *sacerdotes*, "to be appointed"

      Pacullam Anniam Campanam the significance of her Campanian origin is a subject of debate, although Campanians generally do not come off well in Livy.

24-25 **Minium et Herennium Cerrinios** Minius is considered one of the leading men in the conspiracy. Herennius is not mentioned by name again.

pro here, "in place of"

27–28 **sint . . . accesserit** The pres. and pf. subjunctive draw attention to the vividness of Hispala's description.

33–34 **fanatica** Livy also uses this adj. of the adherents of the Magna Mater (38.18.9: *Galli Matris Magnae . . . uaticinantes fanatico carmine*)

Baccharum habitu crinibus sparsis cum ardentibus facibus The description again recalls the Bacchantes of myth and Euripidean tragedy.

35–36 **ad Tiberim** By having Hispala name the Tiber, Livy suggests that these cult practices are a violation of Rome's very landscape.

uiuum sulpur naturally pure sulphur, which does not require refining before use

37–38 **machinae inligatos** A *machina* is, here, a cage or pen for confining someone for the purpose of torture. Cicero says that the Carthaginians confined Regulus to just such a pen before killing him by preventing him from sleeping (*in Pis.* 43: *M. Regulus, quem Carthaginienses . . . inligatum in machina uigilando necauerunt*, "M. Regulus, whom the Carthaginians . . . bound").

39–40 **multitudinem ingentem, alterum iam prope populum esse** In the speech that follows, the consul emphasizes the threat posed by a second populace.

41 **Biennio proximo** "in the last two years"

42 **aetates** here "age groups"

The consul's speech, 39.15.1–14

In 39.14, the consul Postumius asks his mother-in-law to provide Hispala a safe haven. Aebutius is given refuge in the house of one of the consul's clients. Postumius then brings the matter of the cult before the Senate, which authorizes both consuls to hold a special inquiry into it. The Senate also decrees that the priests of the cult be sought out both in Rome and in all market towns and population-centers, that meetings of the cult be publicly banned, and that an inquiry be held regarding anyone who has assembled for any immoral purpose.

Then, in a short passage that nicely illustrates the orderly administer-
ing of a well-functioning government, Livy describes how the consuls
send the curule aediles to put the priests of the cult under house-ar-
rest; they also order plebian aediles to prevent the secret practice of
the cult; the three magistrates in charge of order in the city (*triumviri
capitales*) are authorized to arrange watches guarding against nocturnal assembly and arson; and each of them, in turn, is assigned five
assistants responsible for the buildings in his own district.

The consuls then call an assembly. Since Postumius has played
such an important role in the story, it is probably he who delivers the
speech that follows. But Livy does not name him, perhaps in order to
suggest that the office, not the individual man, is what matters. The
consul begins by emphasizing the importance of traditional prayer
and the traditional gods. He claims that he does not want to say too
much for fear of terrifying his audience; yet his listeners must learn
what kind of people make up this cult. He then portrays the followers of Bacchus as depraved and debauched, and their nocturnal gatherings as illegal. A series of rhetorical questions follows.

1   **haec officia** the duties described by Livy in 39.14

2   **contione aduocata** Who could call an assembly? A magistrate
       or a priest, but not the priests of an unsanctioned foreign cult.
       One of the anxieties that the magistrates feel, and which this
       speech aims to raise in its audience, is that of another city
       forming within Rome, one with its own assemblies and thus a
       threat to the legitimate government.

2–3   **sollemne carmen precationis** "the ceremonial formula of
       prayer"

3–4   **quod praefari solent . . . magistratus** This seems like un-
       necessary information for a Roman reading audience, but the
       consul's first words make it clear why Livy has included it.

5   **Quirites** the name for the Roman people used in especially
       solemn addresses

6   **haec sollemnis deorum comprecatio** a variation on *sollemne
       carmen precationis*

7–8   **hos esse deos, quos ... non illos, qui ...** "*these* are the gods whom ... not *those*, who ..."

          colere uenerari precarique "to worship, revere, and invoke in prayer"

8   **maiores uestri** The idea of "your ancestors" is an important theme in this speech.

          prauis et externis The adj. *prauus* means "crooked" or "awry," then, metaphorically, "depraved."

9   **furialibus stimulis** "the goads of the Furies." The metaphor encompasses the feminine, the chthonic, the irrational, and the foreign.

10–13   Although Postumius says that he does not want to terrify his audience, his words create a sense of foreboding.

11   **quatenus proloquar** "to what extent I should give voice to my thoughts"

12–13   **ne ... dem ... ne ... offundam** two clauses of fearing, with *uereor*

14   **minus quam pro** + abl. "less than is in accordance with"

          scitote The fut. imperative, instead of pres., is regular with *scio*.

15   **dabitur opera** *operam* + *dare*, to devote one's attention (sometimes with dat. of a task, but also, as here with *ut, ne*)

16   **iam pridem** "long ago," "well before now"

18   **crepitibus ... ululatibusque** "clashings" from instruments (drums and rattles), and "howlings" from the mouths of the revelers

19   **certum habeo** introduces indirect speech: *accepisse uos ... ignorare: alios ... alios ... credere*

20   **concessum ludum et lasciuiam** "festival and jollity that is permitted"

21–22   **Quod ad ... attinet** "as far as their number is concerned"

24–27   **Primum ... deinde** The sentence structure reflects the cult's incremental growth.

24-25 **is fons mali** The demonstrative *is* has been attracted into the gender of *fons*.

fuit This *was* the source of evil; the situation has changed.

simillimi feminis mares N.B. *mares*, "males," not *uiri* "men"

26 **constupratores** "defilers." The noun appears here only. Livy also uses the verb *constuprare*.

fanatici The first meaning is "of or belonging to a temple" (*fanum*); the second, in play here, is "inspired by orgiastic rites"

28 **quod . . . fiunt** The emphasis on the cult's steady growth adds urgency

29-30 **uexillo in arce posito** The *uexillum* is a military standard consisting of a piece of cloth suspended from a cross-pole.

comitiorum causa for the sake a meeting at which the Roman citizenry, voting by centuries, the *comitia centuriata*, elected magistrates and priests

30-31 **aut plebi concilium tribuni edixissent** the tribunes had the authority to summon the plebeian assembly

32 **forte temere** a common pairing of the advs. to express chance: "haphazardly"

33 **rectorem** a person in charge

34-35 **Quales primum nocturnos coetus, deinde promiscuos . . . creditis** The description of the gatherings (*coetus*) reflects the growth in the cult described in 24–25, above.

37-41 **Hoc . . . his . . . hi** a series of rhetorical questions, each beginning with the demonstrative pron. The fear Postumius now raises is not that these people will attack but that they will be unable, ever, to defend or fight for Rome.

sacramento in contrast to the customary military oath

sacrario a figurative use of *sacrarium*, a shrine in which religious objects (*sacra*) are kept

ferro metonomy for "the sword" as the instrument of fighting

The consul's speech (continued), 39.16.1–13

The consul points out that the misdeeds of the followers of Bacchus are bringing about not only their own moral ruin. The strength of the cult is limited so far, but growing daily. Left unchecked, its criminal behavior will affect the entire city. As a perverse (*praua*) religion, the cult of Bacchus threatens Rome's good relationship with its traditional gods. Roman magistrates have been tireless in warding off foreign rites in the past, and the consul promises that they will do so energetically in this situation as well.

1   **Minus** sc. *malum*

         flagitiis tantum "by shameful acts alone"

         forent = *essent*

2–3   **ipsorum . . . dedecus erat** *ipsorum* is poss. gen. "that was in a great part their own disgrace"

         <et> added rightly, I think, by Walsh, editor of the text printed here

         a facinoribus manus, mentem a fraudibus Note the chiasmus of both words and initial consonents; a *facinus* is a misdeed, outrage, or crime; *fraudibus* refers to the perjury, forgery, and false witness mentioned at 39.8.7 in the initial description of the cult.

5–6   **Quidquid . . . quidquid . . . quidquid** The anaphora helps the rhetoric swell as Postumius warms to his subject.

6   **ex illo uno sacrario** another figurative use of *sacrarium*

7   **edita facinora habent** *edo* here, in the sense of "to carry out" or "to commit." The pf. pple. with *habere* denotes the continued effect of the action of the verb.

8–9   **priuatis noxiis . . . sese . . . tenet** "maintains itself by means of private wrongdoing"

10   **Crescit et serpit** in the emphatic first position. *Serpit*, "to gain ground gradually," is used of trees spreading as well as of fire, ulcers, and malignant growths.

         capere here, "to give scope for," "to hold"

11   **priuata fortuna** "circumstances that are private." The impor-
        tant word here is *priuata*, as opposed to *publica*.

12–13   **huic diuturnae . . . uocatae** dat. with *par*

        par nocturna contio *par* in pred. position: "a night-time as-
        sembly that is equal"

13–14   **illi uos singuli uniuersos contionantes timent** Latin likes
        to put prons. together: "*they* fear *you*; and *as individuals* they
        fear you *all in assembly*."

14–15   **dilapsi . . . eritis** Used of crowds, *dilabor* means "to slip away
        or disperse"; used of substances such as ice or snow, it means
        "to run away by melting or dissolving" (*OLD* s.v.1). Postumius'
        imagery conveys the importance of social cohesion in this
        face of this threat.

15   **rura uestra** "country-estates"

16–17   **singulis uobis uniuersi timendi erunt** The roles have been
        reversed (cf.13–14).

18   **bona mens** A mind that is sound can resist the *libido* and *fu-
        ror* introduced in the next sentence.

        si quem libido, <si> furor *quem* is in the unemphatic second
        position. The editor retains the second *si* from a late manuscript.

19   **gurgitem** The consul's language remains strongly metaphorical.

20   **flagitium et facinus** our familiar pairing of (sexual) outrage
        and crime

21   **Ne . . . uestrum** clause of fearing after *non sum securus*

        labatur *labor* here, "to be mistaken"

22   **in speciem** "in outward appearance"

23   **praetenditur** "is put forth as a pretext"

23–24   **subit animum timor** introduces another clause of fearing

24   **fraudibus humanis uindicandis** "in punishing human
        crimes"

        diuini iuris partitive gen.

25   **religione** "religious scruple"

27   **Quotiens** How many times *did* this happen? Postumius is
      probably exaggerating, because Livy reports one instance, in
      25.1.6–12.

      hoc with *negotium* looks ahead to *uti . . . uetarent . . . prohibe-
      rent . . . conquirent comburerentque . . . abolerent*

28   **sacra externa** "foreign rites"

29   **sacrificulos uatesque** A *sacrificulus* is a priest in charge of
      sacrifices; a *uates* is a prophet.

      foro circo urbe tricolon, with asyndeton. The last term en-
      compasses the first two; "the forum, the circus (in short), the
      city."

30   **uaticinos libros** In Book 40.29, Livy tells of ancient books
      found in a trunk unearthed by a farmer plowing on the Janic-
      ulum. An inscription on the trunk said that they were books
      of Numa Pompilius, the second king of Rome. Seven, in Latin,
      contained priestly laws, another seven, in Greek, related a sys-
      tem of philosophy. The city praetor determined that they were
      detrimental to religion and, taking his word, the Senate had
      the books burned in the Comitium.

      conquirerent comburerentque The prefix *con-* here connotes
      intensity of action.

      disciplinam here, probably, "system" or "practice"

31   **praeterquam more Romano** "except if done in the Roman
      manner"

34   **nihil aeque . . . quam ubi . . .** "nothing so . . . as when . . ."; *dis-
      soluendae religionis* is predicative gen.

36   **superstitio** here, a disparaging term applied to foreign reli-
      gious practices

37–38 **demolientes nos . . . discutientesque** This is vivid metaphori-
      cal language; the consuls themselves will hardly be wielding
      axes and crowbars.

39   **[ea]** bracketed as an unnecessary direct object of the abl. abso-
      lute *dis propitiis uolentibus*

40–42   **ex occultis ea tenebris in lucem extraxerunt** The gods' actions, too, are presented metaphorically.

nec patefieri . . . uoluerunt introduces the purpose clauses

43–46   **Senatus . . . mandauit. Nos . . . mandauimus** The proper exercise of power in a crisis moves in orderly fashion from the center, the Senate, to the periphery, the people, via the consuls and the minor magistrates.

quaestionem extra ordinem "an exceptional judicial investigation"

48   **impigre praestare** As the consuls act *impigre* (line 44, above), so they expect the people to act; attitude as well as command must emanate from the center.

49   **periculi aut tumultus** partitive gens. dependant on *quid*

After this passage Livy's text goes on to describe the restrictions imposed upon the cult and the severe punishments meted out to the participants. Some were imprisoned, others, who had born false witness or forged wills, or who had become "defiled" (*uiolati . . . contaminati*), were executed. Comparison with the text of the bronze copy of the Senate's decree, the *Senatus Consultum de Bacchanalibus* (**CIL 1.2.622 =ILS* 18; see **Fig. 1**), reveals that some of Livy's language in this description corresponds to that of the Senate's decree. We do not know whether or not Livy saw a copy of the decree himself; but, given his usual practice of relying on earlier historians rather than documentary evidence, it is likely that he based his account on that of a Latin annalist who had used the decree.

*CIL = Corpus Inscriptionum Latinarum   Berlin 1863–
ILS = Inscriptiones Latinae Selectae   Dessau, Berlin 1892–1916

Fig. 1. *Senatus Consultum de Bacchanalibus.* Bronze copy;
Kunsthistorisches Museum, Vienna.

Illustration Credits

Fig. 1. *Senatus Consultum de Bacchanalibus* (*CIL 1.2.622 =ILS* 18). Kunsthistorisches Museum, Vienna.

Fig. 2. (Appendix A) Map: Rome and Its Surroundings. Mapping Specialists, Ltd. © 2011, Bolchazy-Carducci Publishers, Inc.

Fig. 3. (Appendix B) Map: The Western Mediterranean World. Mapping Specialists, Ltd. © 2011, Bolchazy-Carducci Publishers, Inc.

Appendix A

∽ *Map: Rome and Its Surroundings*

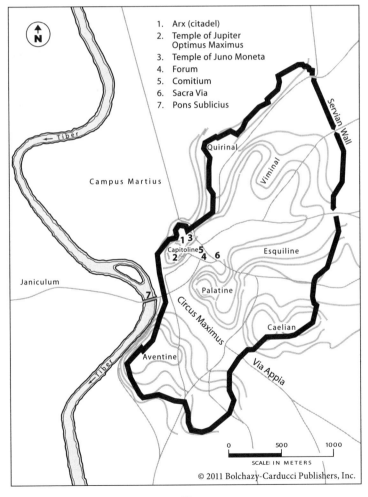

1. Arx (citadel)
2. Temple of Jupiter Optimus Maximus
3. Temple of Juno Moneta
4. Forum
5. Comitium
6. Sacra Via
7. Pons Sublicius

© 2011 Bolchazy-Carducci Publishers, Inc.

Appendix B

⌒ Map: The Western Mediterranean World

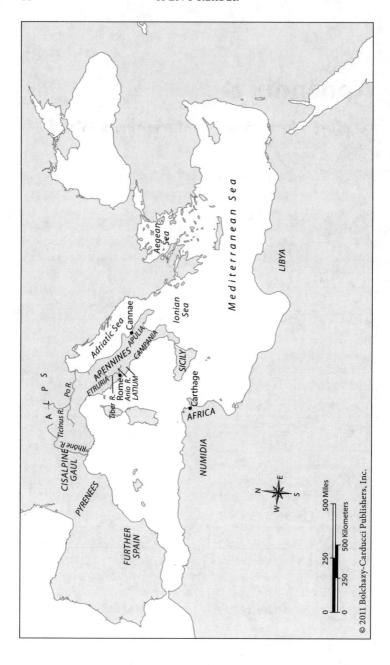

© 2011 Bolchazy-Carducci Publishers, Inc.

Vocabulary

Latin orthography follows that of the *Oxford Latin Dictionary*, ed. P. G. W. Glare, Oxford, 1985 (= *OLD*). When giving several definitions of a word, I have followed the order in which the *OLD* gives them. For some specialized meanings, when the Livy passage is cited by the *OLD*, I have reproduced the exact wording of a definition.

ā *or* **ab,** *prep.* + *abl.*, from; away from; by (*agent*)

abditus, -a, -um, *adj.*, hidden, secret

abdō, -ere, -idī, -itum, to conceal, hide

abeō, -īre, -iī *or* **-īuī, -itum,** to go away, depart

ablēgō (1), to send away; to banish

abnuō, -ere, -ī, —, to refuse to grant; to decline

aboleō, -ēre, -ēuī, -itum, to destroy, obliterate; to dispel; to wipe out

abripiō, -ere, -ipuī, -eptum, to remove by force, snatch away

abrumpō, -ere, -ūpī, -uptum, to break, break apart, rupture

abstineō, -ēre, -uī, abstentum, to keep away; to restrain, hold back

ac. *See* **atque**

accēdō, -ere, -cessī, -cessum, to come to, approach, be added

accendō, -ere, -dī, -sum, to set on fire, kindle; to stir up

accingō, -ere, -nxī, -nctum, to gird (with a sword, etc.); to get ready

accipiō, -ere, -ēpī, -eptum, to receive; to accept as valid

ācer, ācris, ācre, *adj.* sharp, fierce, bitter

aciēs, -ēī, *f.*, a sharp edge; a line of battle

ācriter, *adv.*, forcefully, keenly, attentively

ad, *prep.* + *acc.*, to, towards

addō, -ere, -idī, -itum, to add in, insert; to attach

adeō, *adv.*, to the point (where); to (such) a high degree, (so) very, extremely

adeō, -īre, -iī, -itum, to go to, approach

adfirmō. *See* **affirmō**

adfligō. *See* **affligō**

adhortor, -ārī, -ātus sum, to
encourage, urge

adhūc, *adv.,* so far, as yet,
already, by now

adiciō, -ere, -iēcī, -iectum, to
throw at or towards; to add

adigō, -ere, -ēgī, -actum, to
drive, impel, to bind (a
person by an oath)

adimō, -ere, -ēmī, -emptum, to
remove, take away, deprive of

aditus, -ūs, *m.,* approach

adiungō, -ere, -xī, -ctum, to
connect, join, add (to); to
mention in addition

adloquor. *See* **alloquor**

admīrātiō, -ōnis, *f.,* wonder,
astonishment, surprise

admīror, -ārī, -ātus sum, to be
surprised or astonished (at);
to marvel or wonder (at)

admittō, -ere, -mīsī, -missum,
to admit; to allow; to release

admoneō, -ēre, -uī, -itum, to
remind, give advice to, urge,
warn

admoueō, -ēre, -mōuī, -mōtum,
to move (something) near
(to), bring into contact (with),
lead towards, bring up, apply

adornō (1), to get ready,
prepare, equip

adpetō. *See* **appetō**

adprobō. *See* **approbō**

adscensus. *See* **ascensus**

adsentior. *See* **assentior**

adsuescō. *See* **assuescō**

adsum, adesse, adfuī, —, to be
present; to have come

adsurgō. *See* **assurgō**

adueniō, -īre, -uēnī, -uentum,
to come (to), arrive (at),
reach

aduersus, *prep. + acc.* against,
facing

adulescens, -ntis, *m.* (*f.*), a
youth; a young man or
woman

adulescentulus, -ī, *m.,* a young
man, mere youth

aduocō (1), to call upon,
summon; to call together

Aebutius, -iī, *m.,* Aebutius

aeger, -gra, -grum, *adj.,* ill, sick

aequālis, -is, *m.,* a companion
of one's own age; a
contemporary

aequus, -a, -um, *adj.,* level,
equal, fair, tranquil, calm

aestimō (1), to value; to assess,
judge; to reckon, consider

aetās, -ātis, *f.,* one's age; a
period or time of life

afficiō, -ere, -ēcī, -ectum, to
make an impression upon;
to affect, stir; to afflict

affirmō (1) to add strength to,
confirm

affligō, -ere, -xī, -ctum, to
strike; to demolish; to
damage, impair

Āfrica, -ae, *f.,* continent of
Africa

Āfricus, -a, -um, *adj.,* of Africa,
African

agedum. *See* **agō**

ager, -grī, *m.,* land, territory;
the countryside

agitātiō, -ōnis, *f.,* brandishing, waving, shaking

agitō (1) to set in motion, move, stir, busy oneself, consider

agmen, -inis, *n.,* throng, company, column

agō, -ere, ēgī, actum, to drive; to set in motion; to proceed, deal with; to transact; to debate

agedum *a colloquial imperative,* Come!

āiō, *defective verb,* to say

alacer, -cris, -cre, *adj.,* lively, active, eager, keen

alacritās, -ātis, *f.,* eagerness, zeal

Alba, -ae, *f.,* Alba (Longa)

Albānus, -a, -um, *adj.,* Alban; (*m. pl. substantive*) the inhabitants of Alba

aliēnō (1), to transfer to someone else; to give up

aliēnus, -a, -um, *adj.,* of, or affecting others; not one's own

aliquamdiū, *adv.,* awhile, for some time

aliquis, aliqua, aliquid, *pron.,* someone, something, anyone, anything

aliquō, *adv.,* to some place, somewhere

aliquot, *indecl. adj.,* a number, several, some

alius, -a, -ud, *adj.,* other; **aliī . . . aliī,** some . . . others

alloquor, -ī, -cūtus sum, to speak to, address; appeal to

Alpīnus, -a, -um, *adj.,* of the Alps, Alpine

Alpis, -is, *f., usually pl.* **–ēs, -ium,** the Alps

altāria, -ium, *n.,* an altar for burnt offerings

alter, -tera, -terum, *adj.,* a second; another; the other (of two)

altercātiō, -ōnis, *f.,* a dispute; an argument

āmandō (1), to send away, relegate

amātor, -ōris, *m.,* lover

ambāgēs, -um, *f.,* a roundabout path; evasive speech

ambō, ambae, ambō, *pl. adj. and pron.,* both

āmittō, -ere, -mīsī, -missum, to dismiss, release, give up; to lose in warfare

amnis, -is, *m. and f.,* river

amō (1), to love

amor, -ōris, *m.,* love

āmoueō, -ēre, -mōuī, -mōtum, to cause to go away; to remove

amplus, -a, -um, *adj.,* large, impressive, extensive

an, *particle,* whether; or

anceps, -ipitis, *adj.,* doubtful, dangerous, wavering

ancillula, -ae, *f. diminutive,* a slave girl

angō, -ere, -xī, -ctum, to afflict, vex, cause pain or distress

angustus, -a, -um, *adj.,* narrow, confined, tight

Aniēn, -ēnis, *m.,* the Anio river, a tributary of the Tiber

animaduertō, -ere, -tī, -sum, to pay attention to; to criticize, judge of; to estimate

animus, -ī, *m.*, mind, soul, heart, courage; **in animō mihī est,** "I intend"

Annia, -ae, *f.*, Annia

annus, -ī, *m.*, year

ante, *prep.* + *acc.*, before, in front of

antīquus -a, -um, *adj.*, ancient, early; of olden time

antīquitās, -ātis, *f.*, antiquity, ancient times

anxius, -a, -um, *adj.*, affected with anxiety, worried, uneasy

aperiō, -īre, -uī, -tum, to open, expose; to uncover, reveal

appāreō, -ēre, -uī, -itum, to appear, show up; to become evident

appellō (1), to name; to speak to

appetō, -ere, -īuī *or* **-iī, -ītum,** to desire, strive after; to court

approbō (1), to express approval of, commend

aptus, -a, -um, *adj.*, fitted to, suitable, appropriate

apud, *prep.* + *acc.*, at, near; at the house of; in the presence of

aqua, -ae, *f.*, water

arbitrarium, -(i)ī, *n.*, the power of judging; control, command; authority

arcānum, -ī, *n.*, a secret; a mystery

arceō, -ēre, -uī, to prevent from approaching; to keep away, repulse

ardens, -entis, *adj.*, burning, glowing

arma, -ōrum, *n.*, arms, weapons

armātus, -a, -um, *adj.*, armed

armō (1), to arm, equip

arrectus, -a, -um, *adj.*, upright, steep

ars, artis, *f.*, technical skill, craft

artus, -ūs, *m.*, a joint; an arm or leg, limb

arx, -cis, *f.*, citadel, a strong point in a city

ascensus, -ūs, *m.*, a climbing up, ascent

assentior, -īrī, -sensus sum, to agree, assent, approve

assuescō, -ere, -ēuī, -ētum, to accustom; to become accustomed

assurgō, -ere, -rexī, -rectum, to stand up; to lift oneself; to rise

at, *conj.*, but

atque, *conj.*, and

atrōcitās, -ātis, *f.*, horror, violence, savageness, harshness

attineō, -ēre, -uī, attentum, to hold back, retain, occupy, (with *ad*) to concern, be connected with

attollō, -ere, to raise up, lift up

attonitus, -a, -um, *adj.*, stupified, astounded

auārē, *adv.*, greedily

auctō, -āre, to cause to increase

auctor, -ōris, *m.*, originator, source, person or thing responsible; author

audācia, -ae, *f.*, daring, bravery

audax, -ācis, *adj.*, daring, bold

audeō, -ēre, ausus sum, to dare, be bold

audiō, -īre, -īuī *or* -iī, -ītum, to hear

Auentīnus, -ī, *m.*, *or* Auentīnum, -ī, *n.*, the Aventine hill

augeō, -ēre, -xī, -ctum, to increase, intensify; to extend, amplify

augurium, -ī, *n.*, the taking of auguries (bird omens); an omen, portent, sign

augustus, -a, -um, *adj.*, solemn, venerable, dignified

auis, -is, *f.*, bird

auītus, -a, -um, *adj.*, ancestral, family

aureus, -a, -um, *adj.*, made of gold, golden

auris, auris, *f.*, ear

aurum, -ī, *n.*, gold

aut, *conj.*, or; aut . . . aut, either . . . or

auus, -ī, *m.*, grandfather, ancestor

Baccha, -ae, *f.*, a female votary of Bacchus, a Bacchante

Bacchānalia, -ium, *n.*, a festival of Bacchus, Bacchanalia

Bacchus, -ī, *m.*, Bacchus, a god identified with Dionysus and Liber, and associated with wine

bellum, -ī, *n.*, war; a particular war

bēlua, -ae, *f.*, beast, brute, monster

bene, *adv.*, well, fittingly, favorably

beneficium, -ī, *n.*, a service; a kindness

benignitās, -ātis, *f.*, kindness, benevolence

bīduum, -ī, *n.*, a period of two days

biennium, -ī, *n.*, a period of two years

blandior, -īrī, -ītus sum (*also* -iō), to behave or speak ingratiatingly (to); to coax, flatter, charm

bonus, -a, -um, *adj.*, good

breuis, -e, *adj.*, short, brief, small

C., Gaius

cadō, -ere, cecidī, casum, to be killed, fall (especially in battle)

caedēs, -is, *f.*, killing, slaughter

caelō (1), to adorn; to emboss, engrave

caesim, *adv.*, with a slashing blow

calx, -cis, *f.*, lime

Campānus, -a, -um, *adj.*, Campanian

campus, -ī, *m.*, plain, field

cantus, -ūs, *m.*, singing; a song

capax, -ācis, *adj.*, capable of holding; big enough for

capiō, -ere, cēpī, -tum, to take, appropriate, choose

capitālis, -e, *adj.*, punishable by death, capital

Capitōlium, -ī, *n.*, the Capitoline Hill

captīuus, -ī, *m.*, one taken captive, prisoner of war

captō (1), to grasp at; to catch at

caput, -itis, *n.*, head

cāritās, -ātis, *f.*, dearness, high price; affection

carmen, -inis, *n.*, solemn or ritual utterance; a song

Carthāginiensis, -e, *adj.*, of Carthage, Carthaginian

castimōnia, -ae, *f.*, purity; ceremonial purity, especially by abstinence

castra, -ōrum, *n. pl.*, camp

cāsus, -ūs, *m.*, a fall, end, chance, occurrence

caueō, -ēre, cāuī, -tum, to take precautions, beware, be on one's guard

cauillor, -ārī, -ātus sum, to jest, banter

causa, -ae, *f.*, cause, reason; + *preceding gen.*, for the sake of

-ce, *particle*, (deictic particle added to demonstratives)

cēdō, -ere, cessī, cessum, to withdraw, give ground, fall back

celebrātus, -a, -um, *adj.*, famous, widely known, distinguished

celer, -ris, -re, *adj.*, fast, speedy, quick, agile

Celitibēria, -ae, *f.*, a district occupying the northeastern part of central Spain, Celtiberia

cēlō (1), to conceal, hide

cēnō (1), to dine, eat dinner

censeō, -ēre, -uī, -um, to think, suppose; to recommend

cernō, -ere, crēuī, crētum, to distinguish, discern

certāmen, -inis, *n.*, strife, dispute

certō (1), to contend for superiority; to contend in battle, fight

certus, -a, -um, *adj.*, fixed, settled, sure

ceruix, -īcis, *f.*, neck

cessō (1), to dally, desist; to do nothing, be idle

cēterus, -a, -um, *adj.*, the other, the rest; *n. sing. as adv.*, for the rest, moreover, however that may be

cingō, -ere, -xī, -ctum, to surround, equip, gird

circā, *adv.*, round about; *and prep.* + *acc.*, around, near, about

circumarō, -āre, -āuī, —, to plough around

circumdō, -are, -edī, -atum, to place around

circumferō, -ferre, -tulī,
-lātum, to carry round; to
turn (the eyes, face, etc.) to
face a new direction

circumfundō, -ere, -fūdī,
-fūsum, to pour around,
distribute round; *pass.*, to
spread round, surround

Circumpadānus, -a, -um, *adj.*,
that lies or is situated beside
the Po River

circumscrībō, -ere, -psī,
-ptum, to draw a line
around, restrict, confine

circumsonō, -āre, -uī, -ātum,
to resound all around

circumspectō (1), to look
around

circus, -ī, *m.*, a circular space
in which public games were
held

citātus, -a, -um, *adj.*, made to
move quickly; hurried

citerior, -us, *adj.*, nearer

ciuis, ciuis, *m. and f.*, a citizen

cīuitās, -ātis, *f.*, an organized
community of citizens; a
state

clāmor, -ōris, *m.*, a shout, a cry

clārus, -a, -um, *adj.*, bright,
distinct; celebrated, famous

claudo, -ere, -sī, -sum, to close,
shut up, confine

claudus, -a, -um, *adj.*, lame,
crippled

Cloelia, -ae, *f.*, Roman maiden,
a hostage of Porsenna, who
swam the Tiber

Cocles, -itis, *m.*, Cocles

coeō, -īre, -iī, -itum, to come
together, meet

coepī, -isse, -tum, to begin,
commence

coetus, -ūs, *m.*, meeting,
encounter, gathering

cogitātiō, -ōnis, *f.*, the act
of thinking, reflection;
intention, design

cognitiō, -ōnis, *f.*, the acquiring
or possession of knowledge

cognōmen -inis, *n.*, family or
individual surname, often
derived from some trait or
achievement

cōgō, -ere, coēgī, coactum, to
drive together, collect; to
compel

collēga, -ae, *m.*, conl-, a
colleague, associate

collum, -ī, *n.*, -us, -ī, *m.*, the neck

colō, -ere, -uī, cultum, to live in;
to cultivate, tend, worship

combūrō, -ere, -ussī, -ustum,
to destroy with fire, burn

comes, -itis, *m. and f.*,
companion, attendant

comitium, -ī, *n.*, *comitium*, the
place of public assembly
in the Roman Forum; *pl.*,
an assembly of the Roman
people for the purpose of
electing magistrates

comminus, *adv.*, at close
quarters; hand to hand

committō, -ere, -mīsī, -missum,
to bring into contact (with),
join together, engage (forces)
in battle; to entrust

commoueō, -ēre, -mōuī, -mōtum, to move, rouse

comparō (1), to prepare, get ready, arrange

comprecātiō, -ōnis, *f.,* public supplication or prayers

comprehendō, -ere, -dī, -sum, to unite, seize

concēdō, -ere, -ssī, -ssum, withdraw, submit, hand over; to condone

concilium, -ī, *n.,* a popular assembly; a public meeting or gathering

concursus, -ūs, *m.,* a gathering of a crowd; a running together

condiciō, -ōnis, *f.,* situation, circumstance

conditor, -ōris, *m.,* builder, founder, originator

condō, -ere, -didī, -ditum, to put or insert into, found (a city), establish, put together

conferō, conferre, contulī, conlatum, to convey, direct; to unite, combine, bring together; to oppose

confertus, -a, -um, *adj.,* crowded, dense

conficiō, -ere, -ēcī, -ectum, perform, accomplish, achieve, conclude

confīrmō (1), to strengthen; to assure

congero, -ere, -ssī, -stum, to collect, amass, heap up, assemble

congredior, -ī, -gressus sum, to go near; to approach; to join battle

cōniciō, -ere, -īecī, -iectum, to throw, cast, hurl

coniectō (1), to draw a conclusion about; to judge

coniunx, -ugis, *m. or f.,* husband, wife

coniūrātiō, -ōnis, *f.,* the taking of an oath together, conspiracy, plot

coniūrō (1), to join in taking an oath, form an alliance, join in a plot, conspire

conlēga, *See* **collēga**

cōnor, -ārī, -ātus sum, to undertake, attempt

conquīrō, -ere, -sīuī, -sītum, to search out and collect, hunt down, investigate

consalūtō (1), to greet; to hail (as)

consecrō (1), to dedicate, devote; to regard as divine

consector, -ārī, -ātus sum, to seek, endeavor to obtain, pursue, hunt down

consensus, -ūs, *m.,* agreement

conserō, -ere, -uī, -tum, to join, bring into contact; (*with manum, -us*) to join in battle

consilium, -(i)ī, *n.,* debate, discussion, deliberation, advice

consistō, -ere, -stitī, -stitum, to stop, halt

conspectus, -a, -um, *adj.,* visible, conspicuous

conspectus, -ūs, *m.*, sight, view

constituō, -ere, -uī, -ūtum, to set up, place; to resolve, decide

constō, -āre, -itī, to take up position, stand; to be fixed on, established

constuprātor, -ōris, *m.*, ravisher, defiler

consuētūdō, -inis, *f.*, custom, intimacy

consul, -ulis, *m.*, a consul

consultō (1), to deliberate, debate, consult, discuss

consultum, -ī, *n.*, a decision, resolution, plan, decree

contāgiō, -ōnis, *f.*, infection, pollution

contāminō (1), to spoil, corrupt, pollute

contemptus, -ūs, *m.*, contempt, scorn

conterreō, -ēre, -uī, -itum, to terrify, frighten thoroughly

contiō, -ōnis, *f.*, assembly, meeting

contiōnor, -ārī, -ātus sum, to deliver a public speech; to address a meeting

contundō, -ere, -udī, -ūsum, to crush, bruise, suppress

conualescō, -ere, -uī, —, to grow strong; to recover

conuertō, -ere, -tī, -sum, to cause to turn; to direct one's attention, divert

cooperiō, -īre, -uī, -tum, to cover completely; coopertus + *abl.*, overwhelmed, buried deep

coorior, -īrī, -ortus sum, to spring forth; to break out, arise

cōpia, -ae, *f.*, supply, abundance; *pl.*, supplies

corona, -ae, *f.*, crown

corpus, -oris, *n.*, the body

corruptēla, -ae, *f.*, moral corrupting or perverting

cōtīdiē, *See* cottīdiē

cottīdiē, cōt- quōt-, *adv.*, daily

crēber, -bra, -brum, *adj.*, closely set, frequent

crēdō, -ere, -idī, -itum, to entrust, believe, suppose; *with dat.*, to rely on

creō (1), to create, produce; to elect, appoint

crepitus, -ūs, *m.*, a short sharp sound, cracking, crashing

crescō, -ere, crēuī, crētum, to come into existence; to increase, develop

crīmen, -inis, *n.*, an indictment, charge, accusation

crīnis, -is, *m.*, hair

cruciātus, -ūs, *m.*, torture, severe physical pain

crūdēlis, -e, *adj.*, cruel, merciless, savage

cruentus, -a, -um, *adj.*, bloody

cruor, -ōris, *m.*, blood (from a wound, or spilt in battle)

cultus, -ūs, *m.*, cultivation, worship or veneration

cum, *rel. adv.*, when, since; *prep.* + *abl.*, with

cunctor, -ārī, -ātus sum, to hesitate, delay

cunctus, -a, -um, *adj.*, all

cupīdō, -inis, *f. or m.*,
   passionate desire, longing

cupiō, -ere, -īuī, -ītum, to
   desire, wish for

cūra, -ae, *f.*, trouble, care; +
   esse, to be an object of
   care

custōs, -ōdis, *m. and f.*, guard,
   watch

cymbalum, -ī, *n.*, cymbal

damnō (1), to condemn; *with
   uoti, uoto, etc.*, to oblige to
   fulfill

damnōsus, -a, -um, *adj.*,
   ruinous, detrimental

dē, *prep.* + *abl.*, from, down
   from, about

dea, -ae, *f.*, a goddess

dēbeō, -ēre, -uī, -itum, to
   owe, be indebted, be under
   obligation

dēbilis, -e, *adj.*, feeble, crippled,
   impaired

debilitō (1), to weaken, disable,
   cripple, impair

decem, *adj.*, ten

dēcernō, -ere, -rēuī, -rētum, to
   settle, decide, determine

dēcertō (1), to fight it out,
   contend, compete

decet, -ēre, -uit, to be proper,
   be fitting, be right

decimus, -a, -um, *adj.*, tenth

decōrus, -a, -um, *adj.*, suitable,
   fitting, seemly

dēcrētum, -ī, *n.*, resolve, order,
   decree

dēcurrō, -ere, -cucurrī/-currī,
   -cursum, to run down,
   hurry down

decus, -oris, *n.*, high esteem,
   glory, honor

dēdecus, -oris, *n.*, discredit,
   disgrace, dishonor, shame

dēdō, -ere, -idī, -itum, to give
   up, surrender

dēditus, -a, -um, *adj.*, devoted
   (to); attached (to)

dēdūcō, -ere, -xī, -ctum, to
   lead away, escort,
   accompany

defigō, -ere, -xī, -xum, to fix; to
   attach; to petrify, dumbfound

dēgō, -ere, to spend (one's life,
   etc.); to live

deiciō, -ere, -iēcī, -iectum, to
   throw down; to hurl down,
   drop, cast (as a lot)

dein *or* deinde, *adv.*, then, next;
   henceforth

dēmigrō, (1), to go away from,
   depart

demittō, -ere, -mīsī, -missum
   to let fall; to plunge

dēmōlior, -īrī, -ītus sum, to
   remove, demolish; to do
   away with

dēnique, *adv.*, finally, at last

dens, -ntis, *m.*, tooth

dēposcō, -ere, -poscī, to
   demand

dēprehendō, -ere, -dī, -sum, to
   seize; to catch; to detect

descendō, -ere, -dī, -sum, to go
   down; to get down; to make
   a hostile descent on

dēserō, -ere, -uī, -tum, to abandon, quit; to leave in the lurch

dēsideō, -ēre, -sēdī, to sit idle; to settle

dēsiliō, -īre, -uī, to leap or jump down

dēspērātiō, -ōnis, *f.,* despair, hopelessness (about)

destinō (1), to fix, determine on, intend; to designate, fix on as a target

destituō, -ere, -uī, -ūtum, to abandon, leave alone

dētestor, -ārī, -ātus sum, to call down (a curse on), execrate

dētractō (1), to recoil from; to evade

dētrūdō, -ere, -sī, -sum, to push away, thrust off

deus, -ī, *m.,* god; *pl.,* **dēī/dī/dīī, -ōrum** *or* **deum**

dextrā, *adv.,* on the right (of)

dextra, -ae, *f.,* right hand

dī meliora, *colloquial expression,* god forbid! good god!

dīcō, -ere, -xī, -ctum, to talk, speak; to say, disclose

dictātor, -oris, *m.,* a dictator, a magistrate appointed at Rome for an emergency, and having absolute power for a limited time

diēs, diēī, *m.,* day

differō, -ferre, distulī, dīlātum, to carry off in different directions; to spread abroad; to postpone

difficilis, -e, *adj.,* troublesome, difficult, hard

dignus, -a, -um, *adj.,* suitable, worthy, deserving

dīlābor, -ī, -psus sum, to run, flow away

dīmicō (1), to contend in battle; to fight

dīmittō, -ere, -mīsī, -missum, to send or allow to go away; to release

dīs, dītis, *adj.,* wealthy, rich

discernō, -ere, -rēuī, -rētum, to divide off, distinguish

discerpō, -ere, -psī, -ptum, to tear or rend to pieces

disciplīna, -ae, *f.,* instruction, practice, orderly conduct based on moral training

discrīmen, -inis, *n.,* difference, distinction; decision, critical point

discutiō, -ere, -ssī, -ssum, to shatter; to shake off; to disperse, dispel

dissideō, -ēre -ēdī, to settle apart; to sit awry; to differ, disagree

dissoluō, -ere, -uī, -ūtum, to disintegrate; to undo; to weaken

diū, *adv. compar.* **-ūtius,** for a long time, long

dīues, -itis, *adj.,* wealthy, rich (in)

dīuīnus, -a, -um, *adj.,* of or belonging to the gods or a god, divine

diurnus, -a, -um, *adj.,* of or belonging to the day

dō, dare, dedī, datum, to give

documentum, -ī, *n.*, an example serving as a precedent

dolor, -ōris, *m.*, physical pain; distress, anguish

domesticus, -a, -um, *adj.*, belonging to the home; household

domina, -ae, *f.*, mistress

dominus, -ī, *m.*, master, lord

domus, -ūs *or* **-ī,** *f.*, house, home; **domī militiaeque**, at home and at war

dōnec, *conj.*, until, as long as

dōnō (1), to reward (with); to present, give

donum, -ī, *n.*, gift

dubiē, *adv.*, doubtfully; uncertainly

dubitō (1), to be in doubt, be uncertain; to hesitate

dūcō, -ere, -xī, -ctum, to lead, guide, bring; to consider

ductus, -ūs, *m.*, military leadership, command

dum, *adv.*, yet, now; *conj.*, while (+ *indicative*), provided that (+ *subjunctive*)

duo, -ae, -o, *adj.*, two

duplex, -icis, *adj.*, double

Duronia, -ae, *f.*, mother of P. Aebutius

dux, ducis, *m. or f.*, leader, guide, commander, general

ecquis, -id, *interr. pron. and adj.*, (*in direct question*) Is there anyone/-thing who?; (*in indirect question*) whether anyone or anything

ēdīcō, -ere, -xī, -ctum, to proclaim, decree; to state publicly

ēdō, -ere, -idī, -itum, to emit, bring forth, produce

ēducō (1), to bring up, nurture, rear

ēdūcō, -ere, -xī, -ctum, to lead or bring out

effeminō (1), to emasculate

efferō, efferre, extulī, ēlātum, to carry or bring out or away; to remove

effigiēs (-ēī), *f.*, copy, representation, ghost

effugium, -iī, *n.*, escape; the action of escaping

effundō, -ere, -ūdī, -ūsum, to send forth, bring forth, upset, overturn

ego, meī, *pron.*, I

ēligō, -ere, -ēgī, -ectum, to select, choose

ēmereō, -ēre, -uī, -itum, to serve out, complete (one's term in the army)

ēmētior, -īrī, -nsus sum, to measure out; to pass through or over, traverse; to endure

ēmineō, -ēre, -uī, —, to stand out, be plain or evident

ēmolumentum, -ī, *n.*, advantage, benefit

ēn, *interjection*, see! behold!

ēnecō, -āre, -āuī /-uī, -tum (-ātum), to deprive of life, kill

enim, *particle*, for

ensis, -is, *m.*, a sword

ēnūntiō (1), to make known, disclose; to express

eō, *adv.*, there, to that place

eō, īre, īuī *or* iī, itum, to go, come

epulor, -ārī, -ātus sum, to feast, banquet

eques, -itis, *m.*, a cavalryman; *pl.*, cavalry

equester, -tris, *m.*, equestrian

equidem, *adv.*, (*with first person sing. expressing an implied* ego), I for my part, truly

equus, -ī, *m.*, horse

ergā, *prep.* + *acc.*, next to, towards

ergō, *adv.*, therefore, then

ēripiō, -ere, -puī, -ptum, to seize, snatch away, take by force, carry off

error, -ōris, *m.*, wandering about; deviating from one's path

escendō, -ere, -dī, -sum, to get up (on a platform, etc.), mount

et, *conj.*, and; *adv.*, even, also; et ... et ..., both ... and

etiam, *adv.*, still, yet, even now, also

Etrūria, -ae, *f.*, Etruria

Etruscus, -a, -um, *adj.*, Etruscan; *m. as substantive*, an Etruscan

euentus, -ūs, *m.*, outcome, result, success

ex, *prep.* + *abl.*, from, out of

exaudiō, -īre, -īuī, -ītum, to catch with the ear; to hear

excēdō, -ere, -ssī, -ssum, to go away; to go (beyond specified limits); to proceed beyond (boundaries, etc.)

excidō, -ere, -ī, to fall, drop out; to fall out (be drawn)

excipiō, -ere, -cēpī, -ceptum, to accept, receive

excitō (1), to rouse, stir; to provoke

exemplum, -ī, *n.*, example, specimen, precedent, model

exercitus, -ūs, *m.*, army

exiguus, -a, -um, *adj.*, small, scanty, meagre

eximius, -a, -um, *adj.*, outstanding, exceptional

existimō (1), to value, consider, think

exitus, -ūs, *m.*, a departure, result, outcome

expertus, -a, -um, *adj.*, well-proved, tested

expōnō, -ere, -posuī, -positum, to put out; to abandon, expose

exprōmō, -ere, -psī, -ptum, to bring forth; to disclose

expugnō (1), to capture, subdue

exsecrātiō, -ōnis, *f.*, the act of cursing, imprecation

exsequor, -ī, -cūtus sum, to seek after, pursue; to carry out

ex(s)erō, -ere, -uī, -tum, to thrust out; to show

exsoluō, -ere, -soluī, -solūtum, to loose, free, release

exspirō (1), to breathe out, breathe one's last, die

ex(s)ultātiō, -ōnis, *f*., the action of leaping up and down

exsultō (1), leap about, dance, revel

externus, -a, -um, *adj*., situated on the outside, external, foreign

exterreō, -ēre, -uī, -itum, to scare, terrify

extrā, *prep.* + *acc*., outside of, beyond

extrahō, -ere, -xī, -ctum, to pull out, extract, draw out, bring to light

extrēmus, -a, -um, *adj*., at the end or edge, hindmost, last

fābula, -ae, *f*., talk, tale, legend

facile, *adv*., easily

facinus, -oris, *n*., deed, act; a misdeed, crime

faciō, -ere, fēcī, factum, to do, make, bring about

factum, -ī, *n*., deed, act

Faecinia, -ae, *f*., Faecinia

fallax, -ācis, *f*., deceitful, treacherous, deceptive

fāma, -ae, *f*., report, rumor, reputation

famēs, -is, *f*., hunger, starvation

familia, -ae, *f*., family, household

fānāticus, -a, -um, *adj*., inspired by orgiastic rites; frantic

fās, *n. indecl*., that which is right or permissible by divine law; that which is morally fitting

fax, facis, *f*., torch

fēmina, -ae, *f*., woman

femur, -inis, *n*., thigh

ferē *or* fermē, *adv*., quite, almost

ferō, ferre, tulī, lātum, to carry; to proceed; to endure; to assign, alledge

ferōcia, -ae, *f*., harshness, fighting spirit

ferox, -ōcis, *adj*., having a violent or savage nature, fierce

ferrum, -ī, *n*., iron, sword; "the sword"

fessus, -a, -um, *adj*., tired, weary, exhausted

fidēlis, -e, *adj*., faithful, loyal, trustworthy

fidēs, -ēī, *f*., trust, good faith, credibility

fīgō, -ere, -xī, -xum, to fix in, insert, fasten, secure

fīlius, -ī, *m*., son

fīō, fierī, to be, become, happen

flāgitium, -ī, *n*., a disgrace, a shameful act; an outrage

flamma, -ae, *f*., flame

flūmen, -inis, *n*., a river or stream

foculus, -ī, *m. diminutive*, a small portable stove; a brazier

foedus, -a, -um, *adj*., foul, repulsive, horrible

foedus, -eris, *n*., treaty, compact

fons, -ntis, *m*., a spring; a source, origin

forsitan, *adv.*, perhaps

forte, *adv.*, by chance

fortis, -e, *adj.*, powerful, forceful, bold

fortūna, -ae, *f.*, Fortune (personified); luck, chance, outcome

forum, -ī, *n.*, the public square, the Forum

fouea, -ae, *f.*, pit

fragor, -ōris, *m.*, crash

frangō, -ere, frēgī, -ctum, to break, shatter, smash

frāter, -tris, *m.*, brother

fraudō (1), to deprive a person of what is rightfully his; to cheat

fraus, -dis, *f.*, harm, crime, trickery, deception

frēnātus, -a, -um, *adj.*, wearing a bridle, bridled

frīgus, -oris, *n.*, cold, chill

frūgifer, -fera, -ferum, *adj.*, fruitful, productive, profitable

frūmentum, -ī, *n.*, grain

frustror, -ārī, -ātus sum, to deceive; to escape, elude

fuga, -ae, *f.*, taking flight, fleeing, flight

fugiō, -ere, fūgī, to flee, run away from

fundō, -ere, fūdī, fūsum, to pour, send forth in a stream; (*military*) to rout

furiālis, -e, *adj.*, of or belonging to the Furies, frenzied

furor, -ōris, *m.*, violent madness, hostile rage, fury

furtum, -ī, *n.*, robbery, theft

Gallicus, -a, -um, *adj.*, of Gaul, Gallic

Gallus, -ī, *m.*, a Gaul

gaudium, -iī, *n.*, joy, delight, gladness

gelū, -ūs, *n.*, frost, ice, snow

geminus, -a, -um, *adj.*, twin

gener, -rī, *m.*, son-in-law

generōsus, -a, -um, *adj.*, of noble birth; noble-spirited

gens, gentis, *f.*, race, nation, people; a Roman clan

genus, -eris, *n.*, descent, birth, origin; kind, variety, class; way or method

gerō, -ere, gessī, gestum, to bear, carry, carry on; to perform, do; **bellum gerere,** to wage war

gladius, -ī, *m.*, *also* **gladium, -ī,** *n.*, sword

glōria, -ae, *f.*, praise, honor, distinction

gradus, -ūs, *m.*, step; firm position of the feet

grassor, -ārī, -ātus sum, to march, advance; to prowl

grātia, -ae, *f.*, favor, gratitude

grātulor, -ārī, -ātus sum, + *dat*, to give thanks to; to congratulate

grātus, -a, -um, *adj.*, grateful, thankful; acceptable, welcome

grauis, -e, *adj.*, heavy, weighty; respectable, venerable

gurges, -itis, *m.*, whirlpool, eddy

habeō, -ēre, -uī, -itum, to have, occupy, hold

habilis, -e, *adj.,* easy to handle, easy to control or maneuver

habitō (1), to live in, inhabit

habitus, -ūs, *m.,* condition; expression; state of dress

haereō, -ēre, -sī, -sum, to stick, cling

Hamilcar, -aris, *m.,* Hamilcar Barca, father of Hannibal

Hannibal, -alis, *m.,* Hannibal, the Carthaginian leader in the Second Punic War

haruspex, -icis, *m.,* a diviner

haud, *particle,* not

hauriō, -īre, -sī, -stum, to drain, to draw; to shed (blood)

Hērennius Cerrinius, Hērenniī Cerriniī, *m.,* son of Paculla Annia

hērēs, -ēdis, *m./f.,* heir

Herminius, -iī, *m.,* T. Hermenius, a man who stayed on the bridge with Horatius Cocles

Hibērnus, -ī, *m.,* the Spanish river Ebro

hīc, *adv.,* here, in this place

hic, haec, hoc, *pron. and adj.,* this

hinc, *adv.,* from here, hence

Hispala, -ae, *f.,* Hispala Faecenia, the prostitute involved with P. Aebutius

Hispānia, -ae, *f.,* the Spanish peninsula

Hispānus, -a, -um, *adj.,* Spanish

hōc, *adv.,* to this place, for this reason

homō, -inis, *m. or f.,* man; human being

honōrō (1), to honor

honor (-ōs), -ōris, *m.,* high esteem; a mark of esteem; an honor

hōra, -ae, *f.,* hour

Horātius Cocles, Horātiī Coclitis, *m.,* Roman who held the *Pons Sublicius* against the Etruscans

hostīlis, -e, *adj.,* characteristic of an enemy, hostile

hostis, -is, *m.or f.,* enemy

hūmānus, -a, -um, *adj.,* of or belonging to human beings, human

humus, -ī, *f.,* earth, ground, soil

iaceō, -ēre, -uī, -itum, to lie; lie prostrate; to lie dead

iaciō, -ere, iēci, -tum, to throw, toss

iactātiō, -ōnis, *f.,* tossing, shaking

iam, *adv.,* at this point, now, already

Iāniculum, -ī, *n.,* the Janiculum Hill

ibī, *adv.,* in that place, there; thereupon

īciō *or* **īcō, -ere, -ī, -tum,** to strike with a weapon or missile; to smite

ictus, -ūs, *m.,* a thrust, a blow

īdem, eadem, idem, *pron. and adj.,* the same

identidem, *adv.*, repeatedly

igitur, *conj.*, in that case, then, therefore, consequently

ignārus, -a, -um, *adj.*, ignorant, unaware (of)

ignāuus, -a, -um, *adj.*, lazy, indolent, sluggish

ignis, -is, *m.*, fire

ignōrō (1), to have no knowledge; to be unaware (of)

ignōtus, -a, -um, *adj.*, unknown, unfamiliar, strange

īlicō, *adv.*, on the spot, at once

ille, illa, illud, *pronominal adj,* he, she, it; that

illigō (1), to bind or tie up; to fasten to

illūcescō, -ere, -xī, to begin to grow light

illustris, -e, *adj.*, lighted, bright, clear

illuuiēs, -ēī, *f.*, filthy condition; filth, muck

imāgō, -inis, *f.*, image, likeness, representation, example, model, appearance

imitor, -ārī, -ātus sum, to copy, imitate

immemor, -oris, *adj.*, forgetful

immineō, -ēre, to overhang; to press upon

immisceō, -ēre, -uī, -xtum, to mingle, mix together, confuse

immō, *particle*, rather, more correctly

immolō (1), to offer in sacrifice

immortālis, -e, *adj.*, immortal, undying

immūtō (1), to change, alter

imperātor, -oris, *m.*, a ruler; a commanding officer, general

imperitō (1), to be in command, exercise authority or control (over)

imperium, -ī, *n.*, supreme power, dominion, rule

imperō (1), to give orders to, command

impetus, -ūs, *m.*, a thrust; an attack, assault

impiger, -gra, -grum, *adj.*, active, energetic, brisk

impigre, *adv.*, actively, smartly

impius, -a, -um, *adj.*, showing no regard for moral duties, impious

impōnō, -ere, -posuī, -positum, to put or place in or over; inflict

impūbis, -is, *m.*, a youth; one who has not reached puberty

impūnītus, -a, -um, *adj.*, unpunished

īmus, -a, -um, *adj.*, lowest, bottommost part of

in, *prep. + acc.*, into, onto; + *abl.*, in, on

inaugurō (1), to take the omens by watching the flight of birds

incēdō, -ere, -ssī, to proceed, march forwards, advance

incensus, -a, -um, *adj.*, inflamed

inceptus, -ūs, *m.*, the act of beginning or undertaking; an attempt

incertus, -a, -um, *adj.* doubtful, uncertain

incipiō, -ere, -ēpī, -eptum, to begin

incitāmentum, -ī, *n.*, stimulus, goad

includō, -ere, -sī, -sum, to enclose, confine, hem in, surround

incolumis, -e, *adj.*, unharmed, safe

inconditus, -a, -um, *adj.*, unrefined, crude

incorruptus, -a, -um, *adj.*, intact, unspoiled

incrēmentum, -ī, *n.*, growth, increase

increpitō, -āre, to utter reproaches at, chide, scold

increpō, -āre, -uī, -itum, to chide, rebuke, upbraid

incūsō (1), to blame; to criticize

inde, *adv.*, thence, from that place; from that time

index, -dicis, *m. or f.*, an informer

indicium, -ī, *n.*, information, a sign, evidence

indīcō, -ere, -xī, -ctum, to proclaim, declare

indignē, *adv.*, undeservedly; in an unworthy manner; **indignē ferre,** to take ill, resent

indignitās, -ātis, *f.*, shamefulness, humiliation

indignor, -ārī, -ātus sum, to take offense at, resent, disdain

indignus, -a, -um, *adj.*, unworthy, not deserving

ineō, -īre, -īuī/-iī, -itum, to go into, enter

infandus, -a, -um, *adj.*, unspeakable

infensus, -a, -um, *adj.*, hostile, furious

inferō, inferre, intulī, inlātum, to carry into; to bring forward; to inflict

infestus, -a, -um, *adj.*, hostile, aggressive, threatening

infrēnātus, -a, -um, *adj.*, not using a bridle

ingens, -tis, *adj.*, of very great size, huge, great

inguen, -inis, *n.*, (*also pl.*), the groin

iniciō, -ere, -iēcī, -iectum, to throw in or on

initiō (1), to initiate

initium, -ī, *n.*, beginning; *pl.*, mysteries, sacred rites

iniūria, -ae, *f.*, a wrong, an injustice

iniussū, *m.*, *abl. sing.*, without orders; without leave

inlūcescō. *See* **illūcescō**

inlustris. *See* **illustris**

inluuiēs. *See* **illuuiēs**

innumerābilis, -e, *adj.*, countless, numberless

inopia, -ae, *f.*, want, scarcity

inquam (*with direct speech*), to say

inrīsus, -ūs, *m.*, mockery, ridicule

insequor, -quī, -cūtus sum, to follow closely; to pursue; to follow in time

insideō, -ēre, -ēdī, -essum to
sit, be seated at or on

insidiae, -ārum, *f.,* an ambush;
a treacherous attack

insīgnis, -e, *adj.,* conspicuous,
noteworthy

insimulō (1), to accuse, charge,
blame

insinuō (1), to work one's way in

insistō, -ere, institī, to stand
or tread on; to set about,
proceed with; to stand

instituō, -ere, -uī, -ūtum, to
put up, establish, appoint

insum, inesse, īnfuī, to be in
or on

insuper, *adv. and prep.,* on top,
above, in addition; as well,
over and above

intactus, -a, -um, *adj.,*
untouched, uninjured

integer, -gra, -grum, *adj.,* not
previously touched, whole,
undiminished

intendō, -ere, -dī, -tum, to
stretch, strain, extend, exert

inter, *prep.* + *acc.,* among, amid,
between

intercipiō, -ere, -ēpī,
-eptum, to cut off from its
destination; separate off,
take away

interclūdō, -ere, -sī, -sum, to
fill up, block up; to stop,
choke, stifle

interdiū, *adv.,* during daylight,
by day

interficiō, -ere, -fēcī, -fectum,
to put do death, kill

interior, -us, *adj.,* nearer the
center, closer in (than)

interpres, -etis, *m.,* an
intermediary, interpreter

interrogō (1), ask, to put a
question to

interrumpō, -ere, -rūpī,
-ruptum, to make
discontinous, to break up

interueniō, -īre, -uēnī,
-uentum, to come on the
scene; to intervene, occur,
crop up

intrā, *prep.* + *acc.,* within

intrō (1), to go into, enter

intrōdūcō, -ere, -xī, -ctum, to
lead or bring in

intueor, -ērī, -itus sum, to
look upon, look closely at,
observe

inueniō, -īre, -uēnī, -uentum,
to encounter, find, come
across, discover

inuicem, *adv.,* in exchange, in
turn

inuictus -a, -um, *adj.,*
unconquered, undefeated

inuiolātus, -a, -um, *adj.,* unhurt

inuius, -a, -um, *adj.,*
impassable, inaccessible (*n.*
as substantive)

inūtilis, -e, *adj.,* useless,
unsuitable

ioculor, -ārī, -ātus sum, to jest,
joke

iocus, -ī, *m.,* joke, jest

ipse, -a, -um, *pronominal adj.,*
himself, herself, itself, the
very

īra, -ae, *f.,* anger, rage

īrātus, -a, -um, *adj.,* angry,
enraged

is, ea, id, *pron. and pronominal*
adj., he, she, it; this, that

iste, ista, istud, *pron. and*
pronominal adj., that; that of
yours, that person or thing

ita, *adv.,* to that extent, so, thus

Italia, -ae, *f.,* Italy

itaque, *adv.,* since, in
consequence, so; well then

iter, itineris, *n.,* journey, march,
route, road

iterum, *adv.,* again, once more

iubeō, -ēre, -ssī, -ssum, to
order, command, bid

iūdicō (1), to judge, try, adjudge,
decide

iugulum, -ī, *n.,* throat

iugum, -ī, *n.,* mountain ridge,
pass

iūmentum, -ī, *n.,* beast of
burden

iungō, -ere, -xī, -tum, to join
physically; to bring close
together

iūniōrēs, -um, *m., pl.,* younger
men, especially those of
military age (seventeen to
forty-six years)

iūs iurandum, iūris iurandī,
n., an oath

iūs, iūris, *n.,* law, authority,
right

iustitium, -ī, *n.,* a cessation of
public business

iustus, -a, -um, *adj.,* legitimate,
rightful, fair

iuuenis, -is, *adj.,* young;
substantive m., a young
man

iuuentūs, -ūtis, *f.,* young men
collectively, the youth

iuuō, -āre, iūuī, iūtum, to help,
assist, please

iuxtā, *prep. + acc.,* next to,
beside; in conformity with

L., Lucius

lābēs, -is, *f.,* disaster, debacle

labō, -āre, -āuī, to be shaky,
totter, give way

lābor, -ī, lapsus sum, to slide,
slip, collapse

labor, -ōris, *m.,* work, labor,
toil

lacerō (1), to tear, mangle,
lacerate

Lacrius, Lacriī, *m.,* Sp. Lacrius,
a man who stayed on the
bridge with Horatius Cocles

laetus, -a, -um, *adj.,* happy,
exulting, flourishing

laeua, -ae, *f.,* the left hand

laniō (1), to wound, mutilate,
tear

lapsus, -ūs, *m.,* slipping, falling

lascīuia, -ae, *f.,* play, unruly
behavior, wantonness

lātē, *adv.,* widely, far and wide

Latīnī, -ōrum, *m.,* the
inhabitants of Latium

Latīnus, -a, -um, *adj.,* Latin

laudō (1), to praise, esteem

Lāuīnium, -i, *n.,* Lavinium, a
town in Latium said to have
been founded by Aeneas

lauō, -ere/-āre, lāuī, lautum/ lōtum, to wash, bathe

laus, laudis, *f.,* praise

lēgitimē, *adv.,* lawfully, legitimately, properly

lēgitimus, -a, -um, *adj.,* legal, legitimate, lawful

legō, -ere, lēgī, lectum, to gather, choose, select; to read

lēniō, -īre, -īuī, -ītum, to appease, calm

leuō (1), lift or raise up; to relieve; to free from

lex, lēgis, *f.,* law, the law, a rule

liber, -brī, *m.,* book, document

līber, -era, -erum, *adj.,* free

līberī, -um *or* **-ōrum,** *m. pl.,* children

līberō (1), to free

lībertās, -ātis, *f.,* freedom

lībertīna, -ae, *f.,* freedwoman

libīdō, -inis, *f.,* desire, lust, wantonness

licentia, -ae, *f.,* lack of restraint, disorderliness

licet, -ēre, -cuit/-citum est, *impers.,* it is permitted

lingua, -ae, *f.,* tongue

locō (1), to place

locum *or* **locus, -ī,** *n. or m.,* a place, spot, position; position in society

longē, *adv.,* a long way, far, at a distance

longus, -a, -um, *adj.,* long, extended

loquor, -ī, -cūtus sum, to talk, speak

lūbricus, -a, -um, *adj.,* slippery, hazardous

lūdibrium, -ī, *n.,* playful or insulting treatment, mockery, derision

lūdus, -ī, *m.,* sport, play, game, frivolity

Lūsītānia, -ae, *f.,* the territory of the Lusitani

lux, lūcis, *f.,* light, daylight; **prīmā luce,** at daybreak

māchina, -ae, *f.,* a large mechanism, apparatus

macte *with* **uirtūte esto,** be blessed for your courage; well done

magis, *adv.,* more, rather

magistrātus, -ūs, *m.,* a magistracy; a magistrate

magnitūdō, -inis, *f.,* size, magnitude

magnus, -a, -um, *adj.,* great in size or extent; big

Maharbal, Maharbalis, *m.,* Maharbal, Hannibal's chief cavalry officer

māior, *gen.,* **-ōris,** *n.,* **māius,** *compar. adj.* greater; *m. pl. substantive,* ancestors, forebears

malignē, *adv.,* grudgingly, scantily

malum, -ī, *n.,* trouble, distress, pain, hardship

mandō (1), to hand over, consign, commit, entrust

Manlius, -iī, *m.,* Manlius, name
   of Titus Manlius, son of
   Lucius
manūmittō, -ere, -mīsī,
   -missum, to emancipate; to
   free
manus, -ūs, *f.,* hand, an
   armed force (of any size),
   the power of a husband or
   paterfamilias over his wife
mare, -is, *n.,* the sea
Mars, Martis, *m.,* Italian god of
   war; (*by metonomy*) warfare,
   fighting
mās, maris, *m.,* male
māter, -tris, *f.,* mother
mātrōna, -ae, *f.,* married
   woman, matron
mātūtīnus, -a, -um, *adj.,* of or
   belonging to early morning
maximē, *adv.,* to the greatest
   extent, most, especially, for
   the most part
medium, -iī, *n.,* the middle
   part; the intervening space
melior, -us, *compar. adj.,* better
membrum, -ī, *n.,* part of the
   body, limb
memorābilis, -e, *adj.,* worthy of
   being recorded, remarkable,
   memorable
memoria, -ae, *f.,* the faculty
   of remembering, memory,
   memorial
mens, -tis, *f.,* mind, intention,
   will
mensis, -is, *m.,* month
mercēs, -ēdis, *f.,* payment,
   wage

mereō, -ēre, -uī, -itum /
   mereor, -ērī, -itus sum, to
   earn (*stipendium merere,* to
   draw pay as a soldier); merit;
   deserve, *absolute with adv.,*
   bene, male, *etc., and* **dē +**
   abl., to deserve well, ill, etc.
   (of a person), behave well,
   badly, etc.
meretrīcula, -ae, *f. diminutive,*
   prostitute
mergō, -ere, -sī, -sum, to
   plunge in, dive; to sink in
   the ground, bury
meritum, -ī, *n.,* service;
   something that entitles one
   to a reward
-met, *enclitic particle that adds*
   emphasis
metuō, -ere, -ī, metūtum, to
   fear, be afraid of
metus, -ūs, *m.,* fear
meus, -a, -um, *poss. adj.,* my
mīles, -itis, *m.,* soldier
mīlitāris, -e, *adj.,* of, or
   connected with, the army
mīlitāriter, *adv.,* in a soldierly
   manner
mīlitia, -ae, *f.,* military service,
   war
mille, *indecl. noun and adj., pl.*
   mīlia, a thousand, any large
   number
mināciter, *adv.,* threateningly,
   menacingly
minae, -ārum, *f. pl.,* threats,
   menaces
minimē, *adv.,* in the least degree,
   by no means, not at all

minitābundus, -a, -um, *adj.,*
threatening

Minius Cerrinius, Miniī
Cerriniī, *m.,* son of Paculla
Annia

minor, -us, *adj.,* smaller,
inferior

minus, *compar. adv.,* to a
smaller degree, less

mīrābundus, -a, -um, *adj.,*
wondering, astonished (at)

mīrāculum, -ī, *n.,* an amazing
object or sight; wonder,
amazement

mīrus, -a, -um, *adj.,*
remarkable, astonishing

mīror, -ārī, -ātus sum, to
be surprised, amazed,
bewildered

misceō, -ēre, miscuī, mixtum,
to mix

misereō, -ēre, -uī, to feel or
show compassion, pity, feel
sorry; (*impers.*) *me miseret* +
gen., I am moved to pity

mītis, -e, *adj.,* soft, mild, gentle

mittō, -ere, mīsī, missum, to
release, let go; to discharge;
to send

modicus, -a, -um, *adj.,*
moderate

modo, *adv.,* only, just

modus, -ī, *m.,* way, manner

moenia, -ium, *n. pl.,* city walls,
defensive walls

mōlēs, -is, *f.,* a large mass, a
thing of great size or bulk

moneō, -ēre, -uī, -ītum, to
remind; to warn, advise

monitus, -ūs, *m.,* warning,
omen

mons, -tis, *m.,* mountain, hill

montānus, -a, -um, *adj.,* of or
belonging to the mountains

monumentum, -ī, *n.,*
monument, reminder,
memorial, document, record

mora, -ae, *f.,* delay

morbus, -ī, *m.,* disease, sickness

morior, -ī, mortuus sum, to die

mors, -tis, *f.,* death

mortālis, -is, *m.,* a human
being as opposed to a god

mortuus, -a, -um, *adj.* dead

mōs, mōris, *m.,* custom,
way, manner; *pl.,* morals,
character

mōtus, -ūs, *m.,* motion,
disturbance

moueō, -ēre, mōuī, mōtum,
to move; **signa mouēre,** to
begin a march

mox, *adv.,* in the (near) future,
(a little) later, next

Mūcius, Mūciī, *m.,* Mucius
Scaevola, nobleman who
attempted to kill Porsinna

mucrō, -ōnis, *m.,* sharp point,
end of a sword; sword (in
action)

mulier, -eris, *f.,* a woman, wife;
a mistress

multitūdō, -inis, *f.,* abundance,
multitude, population

multō, *adv.,* much, by far

multus, -a, -um, *adj.,* much,
many

mūnia, *n. pl.,* duties, functions

mūnificentia, -ae, *f.,* bounty, munificence

mūnīmentum, -ī, *n.,* defence, protection

mūrus, -ī, *m.,* (*often pl.*), a wall built for defense, city wall

nam, *conj.,* for, because

nanciscor, -ī, nactus sum, to acquire, get, obtain

nāsus, -ī, *m.,* nose

nāuis, -is, *f.,* ship

nē, *negative adv. and conj.,* so that not, lest; **nē . . . quidem,** not even

nec. *See* **neque**

necdum, *conj., adv.,* and not yet; not yet

necessārius, -a, -um, *adj.,* essential, necessary, critical

necesse, *adv.,* indispensable, essential

necessitās, -ātis, *f.,* need, necessity, constraint, difficulty

nefārius, -a, -um, *adj.,* offending against moral law, wicked

nefās, *n. indecl.,* an impious act, sacrilege

neglegentia, -ae, *f.,* lack of care, carelessness

negōtium, -(i)ī, *n.,* work, business, job

nēmō, -inis, *m. or f.,* no one

nēquāquam, *adv.,* by no means

neque *or* **nec,** *conj., adv.,* and not, nor; **neque . . . neque,** *or* **nec . . . nec,** neither . . . nor

nequeō, -īre, -īuī/-iī, to be unable

nēquīquam, *adv.,* in vain

neruus, -ī, *m.,* sinew, muscle

nesciō, -īre, -iuī/-iī, -ītum, not to know, to be unaware of; **nesciō an,** I am inclined to think

neuter, -tra, -trum, *adj.,* not one or the other, neither

nī, *conj., adv.,* not; that . . . not; unless

nihil, *n. indecl.,* nothing

nihilōminus, *adv.,* none the less

nimirum, *particle,* evidently, of course

nimis, *n. indecl.,* an excessive amount; *adv.,* too much

nimium, -ī, *n.,* an excessive amount or degree, too much, a great amount

nisi, *conj.,* except if, unless

nix, niuis, *f.,* snow

nōbilis, -e, *adj.,* generally known, renowned, famous; aristocratic

nocturnus, -a, -um, *adj.,* of or belonging to the night, nocturnal

nōlō, nolle, nōluī, to be unwilling; not to want

nōmen, -inis, *n.,* name, renown

nōn, *adv.,* not

nōndum, *adv.,* not yet

nōnus, -a, -um, *adj.,* ninth

nos, *pron.,* we

noster, -stra, -strum, *adj.,* our

nouem, *indecl. adj.,* nine

nouus, -a, -um, *adj.,* new

nox, noctis, *f.*, night

noxia, -ae, *f.*, wrongdoing, harm, damage

noxius, -a, -um, *adj.*, guilty, harmful, injurious

nūdō (1), to strip bare, uncover, expose

nullus, -a, -um, *adj.*, none, no

nūmen, -inis, *n.*, divine power or influence, divinity, godhead

numerus, -ī, *m.*, number

Numida, -ae, *m.*, a native of Numidia, Numidian

Numitor, -ōris, *m.*, king of Alba; grandfather of Romulus and Remus

numquam/nunquam, *adv.*, never, at no time

nunc, *adv.*, now

nuntiō (1), to announce, report

nusquam, *adv.*, nowhere; under no circumstances

obiciō, -ere, -iēcī, -iectum, to throw or put before or in the way; *pass.*, to be in the way as a barrier

obnoxius, -a, -um, *adj.*, indebted, under obligation; subservient (to)

obruō, -ere, -ī, -tum, to cover up, bury, submerge; to smother

obscēnus, -a, -um, *adj.*, loathsome, indecent, lewd

obsecrō (1), to beseech, entreat, implore

obseruō (1), to observe; to beware of, watch for; to respect

obses, -idis, *m. or f.*, hostage

obsideō, -ēre, -ēdī, -essum, to besiege, blockade

obsidiō, -ōnis, *f.*, siege, blockade

obsistō, -ere, -stitī, -stitum, to stand in the way, resist, withstand

obstinātus, -a, -um, *adj.*, stubborn, resolute

obstō (1), to be facing, stand in the way, prevent, withstand, oppose

obstupefaciō, -ere, -fēcī, -factum, to astonish, amaze

obtestor, -ārī, -ātus sum, to call upon, invoke; to implore

obtineō, -ēre, -inuī, -entum, to maintain; to hold, occupy

obtruncō (1), to to pieces; to kill

obuertō, -ere, -tī, -sum, to turn so as to face; to turn (weapons, troops) in a hostile way

obuiam, *adv.*, in the way; so as to meet

occāsiō, -ōnis, *f.*, convenient or favorable circumstances, opportunity, chance; **per occāsiōnem,** at a favorable opportunity

occīdō, -ere, -cīdī, -cīsum, to strike down, kill

occidō, -ere, -idī, -āsum, to fall; to die, be struck down; to set (of heavenly bodies)

occultus, -a, -um, *adj.,* secret, concealed

occupō (1), to seize, take possession of

occurrō, -ere, -rrī, -rsum, to run to meet, meet or confront (in a hostile manner), come upon

oculus, -ī, *m.,* eye

odium, -iī, *n.,* feeling of aversion, hatred, dislike

officīna, -ae, *f.,* workshop

officium, -ī, *n.,* service, duty, task

offundō, -ere, -ūdī, -ūsum, to pour or extend (over a surface): to cover; to overwhelm

omnis, -e, *adj.,* all, each, every

opera, -ae, *f.,* task, effort

opīmus, -a, -um, *adj.,* rich, choice

oportet, -ēre, -uit, —, *impers.,* it is proper/right

oppetō, -ere, -īuī/-iī, -itum, to encounter; to meet; to meet one's end, perish

oppleō, -ēre, -ēuī, -ētum, to fill up, cover completely

opportūnus, -a, -um, *adj.,* convenient, advantageous, exposed, susceptible to

opprimō, -ere, -essī, -essum, to press on; to smother, bury; to overpower

oppugnō (1), to attack, assail

ops, opis, *f.,* power, ability, resources, wealth

optimē, *adv.,* most satisfactorily, best

optō (1), to wish for, desire, choose

opulentus, -a, -um, *adj.,* wealthy, rich, valuable

opus, -eris, *n.,* work, labor; the product of work; a literary work; **opus est** (*with abl., gen.*), I have need of

ōrātor, -ōris, *m.,* orator, envoy

ordō, -inis, *m.,* row, line, rank

orīgō, -inis, *f.,* a beginning, origin, source

orior, -īrī, -tus sum, to rise, emerge; to come into existence, be born; to arise

ornātus, -ūs, *m.,* equipment, adornment

ōrō (1), to pray, beseech

ōs, ōris, *n.,* mouth, face

ostendō, -ere, -dī, -tum, to show, display

ostentō (1), to present to view, exhibit, display, show

P., Publius

pācātus, -a, -um, *adj.,* settled, calm, peaceable, subdued

Paculla Annia, Pacullae Anniae, *f.,* priestess of Bacchus

Padus, -ī, *m.,* the river Po

paene, *adv.,* nearly, almost

Palātium, -ī, *n.,* Palatine Hill

pār, paris, *adj.,* equal

pār, paris, *n.,* a set of two; a pair

parcō, -ere, pepercī, to refrain from; to spare (*with dat.*); to be merciful

parens, -entis, *m./f.,* parent

pariō, -ere, peperī, -tum, to
bring forth, produce; to
procure

pars, partis, *f.,* part, portion,
section

parum, *n. indecl. and adv.,*
too little, not enough,
inadequate

parumper, *adv.,* for a short
while, for a moment

paruus, -a, -um, *adj.,* small

passim, *adv.,* here and there, all
over the place; at random

pastor, -ōris, *m.,* shepherd

patefaciō, -ere, -fēcī, factum,
to make visible, reveal,
uncover

pater, -tris, *m.,* father, senator

patiens, -entis, *adj.,* suffering,
enduring, permitting

patior, -ī, passus sum, to
experience, suffer, undergo;
to allow, permit

patria, -ae, *f.,* one's native land

patrius, -a, -um, *adj.,* of or
belonging to a father,
paternal

patrōnus, -ī, *m.,* patron

paucus, -a, -um, *adj.,* (*usually
pl.*), a small number, few, a
little

paueō, -ēre, pāuī, —, to be
frightened, be terrified

paulātim, *adv.,* little by little,
gradually

paulō, *adv.,* by a small amount,
by a little

paulum, *adv.,* only to a small
extent, slightly

pauor, -ōris, *m.,* terror, sudden
fear

pax, pācis, *f.,* peace

peccō (1), to blunder, commit a
fault, do wrong

pectus -oris, *n.,* the chest,
breast (as seat of the
emotions)

pecus, -oris, *n.,* livestock,
especially sheep and cattle

pedes, -itis, *m.,* foot-soldier,
infantryman

pedester, -tris, -tre, *adj.,* going
by foot, (*of weapons*) used by
the infantry

pendēo, -ēre, pependī, to be
suspended, hang

pensō (1), to weigh out; to
ponder, consider

penetrō (1), to enter, penetrate

per, *prep. + acc.,* through;
throughout a period;
through the agency of

peragō, -ere, -ēgī, -actum,
to carry out, perform,
complete

percellō, -ere, -ulī, -ulsum, to
strike down; to strike hard,
hit

perdō, -ere, -idī, -itum, to
cause ruin; to destroy, ruin

perducō, -ere, -xī, -ctum, to
conduct, bring; to convey

pereō, -īre, -iī, -itum, to vanish,
disappear, be lost, perish

perficiō, -ere, -fēcī, -fectum, to
achieve, complete, perform

perfidia, -ae, *f.,* faithlessness,
treachery

perfungor, -ī, -ctus sum, to carry through, be done with

pergō, -ere, -rexī, -rectum, to make one's way; to proceed

perīculum, -ī, *n.,* test, trial, danger

permittō, -ere, -mīsī, -missum, to allow, grant, permit

perniciēs, -ēī, *f.,* destruction, injury, ruin

personō (1), to make a loud noise, resound

pertineō, -ēre, -uī, to extend, reach, relate (to), be a concern (to)

perturbātiō, -ōnis, *f.,* confusion, disturbance, distress

perturbō (1), to upset, agitate, confound

peruenio, -īre, -uēnī, -uentum, to come, arrive (at)

pēs, pedis, *m.,* foot

petō, -ere, -īuī/-iī, -ītum, to reach out for; to make for, seek

pictus -a, -um, *adj.,* painted

pietās -ātis, *f.,* attitude of dutiful respect

piger, -gra, -grum, *adj.,* sluggish, torpid

pīgnus, -eris/-oris, *n.,* a pledge; a hostage

pigritia, -ae, *f.,* sluggishness

plānus, -a, -um, *adj.,* level, flat

plebs, -ēbis, *f.,* the plebeian class, the commons

plēnus, -a, -um, *adj.,* full

plērusque, -aque, -umque, *adj.,* the greater part or number of, most of; **plērique omnēs,** nearly all

plūs, plūris, *n.,* more

Poenus, -a, -um, *adj.,* Phoenician, Carthaginian, of Carthage

poēticus, -a, -um, *adj.,* belonging to or suited to poetry

pōnō, -ere, posuī, positum, to put, place, set

pons, -ntis, *m.,* bridge

pontifex, -icis, *m.,* one of the college of priests with supreme control in religious matters

poples, -itis, *m.,* knee

populātiō, -ōnis, *f.,* plundering, spoiling

populus, -ī, *m.,* a people, nation, the general public, a crowd

porrigō, -ere, -exī, -ectum, to stretch out, lay prostrate, cause to spread out

Porsinna, -ae, *m.,* Lars Porsinna, the Etruscan king who laid siege to Rome

poscō, -ere, poposcī, to ask for insistently, demand

possessiō, -ōnis, *f.,* occupancy, seizure, control

possideō, -ēre, -ēdī, -essum, to hold, occupy, possess, have control of

possum, posse, potuī, to be able

post, *prep. + acc.,* behind, after

posterus, -a, -um, *adj.*, next, subsequent; *pl.*, coming generations, descendants

postquam, *conj.*, after; ever since

Postumius, -ī, *m.*, Sp. Postumius Albinus, consul in 186 BCE

potestās, -ātis, *f.*, command, control, power

potior, -īrī, -tītus sum, to take possession, to obtain (*with acc., gen., or abl.*)

potis, *adj. indecl.*, able, capable

potissimum, *adv.*, especially, above all

potius, *adv.*, rather, more than

prae, *adv.*, before

prae, *prep.* + *abl.*, before, in comparison with

praebeō, -ēre, -uī, -itum, to offer, make available, provide

praecaueō, -ēre, -cāuī, -cautus, to be on one's guard, beware, take precaution

praecēdō, -ere, -essī, -essum, to go in front of, come before, precede

praeceps, -cipitis, *adj.*, headlong, falling steeply, sheer

praecipiō, -ere, -cēpī, -ceptum, to forestall, take first, anticipate

praecipitō (1), to cause to fall headlong; to hurl down

praecipuē, *adv.*, chiefly, principally

praecipuus, -a, -um, *adj.*, peculiar, special, outstanding

praedicō (1), to proclaim, declare

praedō, -ōnis, *m.*, a robber, brigand

praefectus, -ī, *m.*, the officer in command (of)

praefor, -ārī, -ātus sum, to say beforehand or by way of preface, mention first

praegredior, -ī, -ssus sum, to go ahead, go in front

praemium, -ī, *n.*, payment, reward, prize

praesidium, -ī, *n.*, defense, protection; a stronghold

praestō, -āre, -itī, -ātum, to furnish; (*with predicate adj.*) to keep (*safe, etc.*)

praesultō, -āre, to dance in front of

praetendō, -ere, -dī, -tum, to hold out; to put forth as pretext

praeter, *prep.* + *acc.*, besides, other than

praetereā, *adv.*, as well, besides, furthermore

praetermittō, -ere, -mīsī, -missum, to disregard; to leave out

praeterquam, *conj.*, apart from, except, beyond

praetor, -ōris, *m.*, praetor; a Roman magistrate concerned chiefly with judicial functions

praeūrō, -ere, -ussī, -ustum, to scorch or freeze at the extremity

prāuus, -a, -um, *adj.,* crooked, corrupt, perverse

precātiō, -ōnis, *f.,* an act of supplication, prayer

precor, -ārī, -ātus sum, to ask or pray; to beg, implore

pretium, -ī, *n.,* reward, prize

prīdem, *adv.,* some time ago, formerly; with iam, long ago

prīmō, *adv.,* at first

prīmordium, -ī, *n.,* beginning, origin, source

primōrēs, -um, *m. pl.,* the front ranks

prīmum, *adv.,* first, in the first place; with **ubi,** as soon as

prīmus, -a, -um, *adj.,* first, foremost, uttermost, earliest

princeps, -cipis, *adj.,* first, foremost

principium, -ī, *n.,* a beginning, origination, start

prior, -ius, *compar. adj.,* ahead, earlier, first

prīuātus, -a, -um, *adj.,* private, particular to a person

priusquam, *conj., also* **prius . . . quam,** before

prō, *prep.* + *abl.,* in front of, in place of, on behalf of

probābilis, -e, *adj.,* commendable, acceptable

prōcēdō, -ere, -ssī, -sum, to move forward, advance

procella, -ae, *f.,* tumult, commotion

proceres, -um, *m. pl.,* leading men of a city

prōcidō, -ere, -idī, to fall forward, collapse

proclīuis, -e, *adj.,* sloping down, downward; easy

procul, *adv.,* far, at a distance, far away, far

prōdūcō, -ere, -xī, -ctum, to lead forth, bring out

proelium, -ī, *n.,* an armed encounter, battle

proficiscor, -ī, profectus sum, to set out

profiteor, -ērī, -essus sum, to state openly, declare, avow, promise

prōflīgō (1), to defeat decisively; perform the greater part of ("break the back of") a task

prōgredior, -ī, -ssus sum, to go forwards, advance, proceed

prohibeō, -ēre, -uī, -itum, to keep off, exclude, prevent, forbid

prōiciō, -ere, -iēcī, -iectum, to throw or fling forth; to extend

proinde, *adv.,* accordingly

prōlābor, -ī, -psus sum, to slide or slip forth, drop, collapse

prōloquor, -quī, -cūtus sum, to speak forth, announce, reveal

prōmiscuus, -a, -um, *adj.,* possessed by each equally; **in prōmiscuō,** with no distinction

prōmunturium, -(i)ī, *n.,* promontory, headland
prope, *adv.,* near; *prep. + acc.,* near, by
properē, *adv.,* quickly
properō (1), to hasten, go quickly
propinquus, -a, -um, *adj.,* close, neighboring; (*as substantive*), kinsman
propior, -ius, *compar. adj.,* nearer, closer, earlier, more recent
propitius, -a, -um, *adj.,* favorably inclined; well disposed
prōpōnō, -ere, -posuī, -positum, to expose to view, exhibit; to set up, place before; to offer
prōsiliō, -īre, -uī, to spring forward, rush forth
prospectus, -ūs, *m.,* prospect, view, outlook
prōtegō, -ere, -xī, -ctum, to cover, protect, defend
prōuocō (1), to call out, challenge
prōuincia, -ae, *f.,* a province
proximus, -a, -um, *adj.,* the nearest
prūdens, -ntis, *adj.,* well aware; open-eyed; discreet
pūblicus, -a, -um, *adj.,* of the people, common to all
Publius Aebūtius, Publiī Aebūtiī, *m.,* Roman who helped expose the Bacchanalia

pudeō, -ēre, -uī (*or impers.,* **-itum est**), to make ashamed, be ashamed (*impers. with acc. of person and gen. of cause of shame*)
pudīcitia, -ae, *f.,* sexual purity, chastity, virtue
pudor, -ōris, *f.,* shame, sense of decency
puerīliter, *adv.,* boyishly, childishly
pugna, -ae, *f.,* fight, battle
pugnō (1), to contend in battle, fight
pulsus, -ūs, *m.,* the action of beating; a beat or stroke
Pūnicus, -a, -um, *adj.,* of Carthage, Carthaginian, Punic
pūpillus, -ī, *m. diminutive,* ward, orphan
pūrē, *adv.,* with ritual purity
putō (1), to ponder, think, consider

quā, *interr., indef., and rel. adv.,* by which route, where
quaerō, -ere, -sīuī, -sītum, to search for, make inquiries, ask
quaestiō, -ōnis, *f.,* examination, investigation, inquiry
quaestus, -ūs, *m.,* pursuit, occupation
quālis, -e, *interr. and rel. adj.,* of which sort or quality, such as
quāliscumque, -ecumque, *rel. adj.,* of whatever sort or quality, whatever

quam, *adv.,* how; than

quandō, *adv.,* at which time; when; seeing that

quantum, *interr. and rel. adv.,* how greatly? to what extent, degree

quantus, -a, -um, *rel. adj.,* how much, as much as

quasi, *adv.,* as if, just as

quassō (1), to shake repeatedly; to batter, bruise

quātenus, *interr. and rel. adv.,* how far? to the extent that

-que, *enclitic conj.,* and

quemadmodum, *interr. and rel. adv.,* in what way

quī, quae, quod, *rel. pron. and adj.; interr. pron.,* who, which, what; *indef. adj.,* any

quia, *conj.,* since, because

quīcumque, quaecumque, quodcumque, *rel. and indef. pron. and adj.,* whoever, whatever

quīdam, quaedam, quoddam, *indef. pron.,* a certain; a certain one, somebody

quidem, *adv.,* indeed, certainly

quiēs, -ētis, *f.,* rest, relaxation

quīn, *conj.,* that not, in fact

quīnī, -ae, -a, *pl. adj.,* five each, five apiece

quinque, *indecl. adj.,* five

quintus, -a, -um, *adj.,* fifth

Quirītēs, -ītium, *m. pl.,* a name given to the citizens of Rome, especially in solemn addresses

quirītō, -āre, to cry in protest

quisquam, quicquam, *indef. pron.,* anyone, anything

quisque, quaeque, quidque, *indef. adj. and pron.,* each, each one

quisquis, quidquid, *pron. and adj.,* whoever, whatever

quō, *adv.,* where

quoad, *interr. and rel. adv.,* to what extent; as long as, until

quōcumque, *rel. adv.,* to any place, wherever

quod, *rel. adv.,* as to which, inasmuch as, as to the fact that, because

quondam, *adv.,* once, formerly

quoniam, *conj.,* seeing that; since

quoque, *adv.,* besides, as well

quōtīdiē, *See* **cottīdiē**

quotiens, *rel. adv.,* as often, whenever, the number of times that

rabiēs (-ēī), *f.,* savageness, ferocity, madness

rapiō, -ere, -uī, -tum, to seize and carry off; to snatch away

raptim, *adv.,* hurriedly, hastily, in a rush

ratiō, -ōnis, *f.,* a reckoning, calculation; the act of reasoning

recens, -ntis, *adj.,* lately done or made, recent

reciperō (1), to recover, get back, restore

recipiō, -ere, -ēpī, -eptum,
to admit, receive, allow
to enter; (*with reflex.*)
withdraw, retire

rector, -ōris, *m.*, a helmsman,
ruler, governor, controller

reddō, -ere, -idī, -itum, to
give back, render; **rationem
reddere,** to render an
account

redintegrō (1), to restore,
renew

refellō, -ere, -fellī, to refute,
disprove

referō, -ferre, rettulī, relātum,
bring back; to report, record;
to pay as due, render

refulgeō, -ēre, -sī, to shine
brightly; to flash

rēgia, -ae, *f.*, a royal residence,
palace

rēgius, -a, -um, *adj.*, royal,
kingly

rēgnum, -ī, *n.*, kingship,
dominion, rule

regō, -ere, rexī, rectum, to
direct, guide, control,
command

religiō, -ōnis, *f.*, a supernatural
feeling of constraint;
religious practice, custom

relinquō, -ere, -līquī, -lictum,
to depart from; to leave
behind

reliquiae, -ārum, *f. pl.*,
remnants, remains

reliquus, -a, -um, *adj.*, left,
remaining

remedium, -ī, *n.*, remedy, care

remittō, -ere, -mīsī, -missum,
to send back, return

remūneror, -ārī, -ātus sum, to
repay

Remus, -ī, *m.*, brother of
Romulus

reor, -ērī, ratus sum, to think,
suppose

repentīnus, -a, -um, *adj.*,
sudden

reprehendō, -ere, -dī, -sum,
to hold back; to censure,
rebuke

reputō (1), to think over, bear in
mind, consider

rēs, reī, *f.*, property, thing,
affair, deed; *pl.*, exploits

rēs pūblica, reī pūblicae, *f.*,
republic

rescindō, -ere, -idī, -scissum,
to remove by cutting; to cut
or tear open

respectus, -ūs, *m.*, safety, refuge

respergō, -ere, -sī, -sum, to
sprinkle, splash, splatter

respondeō, -ēre, -dī, -sum, to
answer, reply

responsum, -ī, *n.*, answer, reply,
answer given by an oracle or
soothsayer

restituō, -ere, -uī, -ūtum, to set
up; to restore

retrahō, -ere, -xī, -ctum, to
drag back; to compel to
return

reuocō (1), to call back, call off

rex, rēgis, *m.*, king

Rhodanus, -ī, *m.*, the river
Rhone

rigeō, -ēre, to be stiff, rigid; to be numb with cold

rīpa, -ae, *f.,* bank (of a river)

rītus, -ūs, *m.,* religious rites, ceremonies; *abl. sing. with adj.,* according to a given rite

rōbur, -oris, *n.,* physical strength, vigor, military power

Rōma, -ae, *f.,* Rome

Rōmānus, -a, -um, *adj.,* Roman, of Rome

Rōmulus, -ī, *m.,* founder of Rome

rostra, rostrōrum, *n. pl.,* the platform from which speakers addressed the people at Rome

rumpō, -ere, rūpī, ruptum, to cause to break (open, down); to rupture; to break

ruō, -ere, -ī, to move swiftly, to rush headlong; to fall, collapse

rūpēs, -is, *f.,* steep rocky cliff, crag

ruptor, -ōris, *m.,* one who breaks or violates (an agreement)

rūs, rūris, *n.,* country, land, country estate

sacer, -cra, -crum, *adj.,* sacred

sacerdōs, -ōtis, *m./f.,* priest, priestess

sacrāmentum, -ī, *n.,* an oath; a military oath of allegiance

sacrārium, -ī, *n.,* shrine, sanctuary

sacrificium, -ī, *n.,* sacrifice

sacrificō (1), to perform a sacrifice, offer up as a sacrifice

sacrificulus, -ī, *m.,* a sacrificial priest

sacrum, -ī, *n.,* a sacred object; a holy place; a religious ceremony

saepe, *adv.,* often, frequently

saepiō, -īre, -psī, -ptum, to surround

Saguntīnus, -a, -um, *adj.,* of Saguntum or its inhabitants; *as substantive m. pl.,* the people of Saguntum

Saguntum, -ī, *n.,* Saguntum, a town in Hispania Tarraconensis

salūber, -bris, -bre, *adj.,* healthy, beneficial

salūs, -ūtis, *f.,* safety, welfare

sānctus, -a, -um, *adj.,* sacrosanct, inviolate, holy

sanguis, -inis, *m.,* blood

Sardinia, -ae, *f.,* the island of Sardinia

satelles, -itis, *m./f.,* bodyguard, henchman

satis, *n. indecl. substantive* enough; *adv.,* enough, sufficiently; *compar.,* **satius,** better

saxum, -ī, *n.,* stone, rock

scelus, -eris, *n.,* a crime, villainy, affliction

sciō, -īre, -īuī, -ītum, to know, understand

sciscitor, -ārī, -ātus sum, to ask, inquire

scortum, -ī, *n.*, prostitute

scrība, -ae, *m.*, secretary

scrībō, -ere, -psī, -ptum, to inscribe, write, make a record of, compose

scriptor, -ōris, *m.*, one who writes; writer of literary works (*with gen. of subject matter*)

scūtum, -ī, *n.*, shield

sē, sēsē, *reflex. pron.*, himself, herself, itself

sēcrētus, -a, -um, *adj.*, secret, hidden

sēcubō, -āre, -uī, to sleep apart from one's spouse or lover

secundum, *prep. + acc.*, behind, after, along

sēcūrus, -a, -um, *adj.*, free from care, untroubled

sed, *conj.*, but

sedeō, -ēre, sēdī, sessum, to sit; (of an army) to remain encamped

sēdēs, -is, *f.*, seat, throne

segniter, *adv.*, without energy, half-heartedly, feebly

sēmet, *a strengthened form of* **sē**

Semprōnius Rutilus, Semprōniī Rutilī, *m.*, T. Sempronius Rutilus, the step-father of P. Aebutius

senātus, -ūs, *m.*, the Senate

sensus, -ūs, *m.*, a sensation

sentiō, -īre, -sī, -sum, to perceive, understand

sequor, -ī, secūtus sum, to follow, attend upon

sērius, -a, -um, *adj.*, weighty, important, serious

sermō, -ōnis, *m.*, speech, talk, conversation

serpō, -ere, -sī, to crawl, glide; to gain ground gradually

seruiō, -īre, -īuī/ iī, -ītum, to be enslaved, serve

seruitium, -ī, *n.*, slavery, servitude; *pl.*, slaves

sex, *adj.*, six

sī, *conj.*, if

sīc, *adv.*, thus, in this way; so

Sicilia, -ae, *f.*, the island of Sicily

sīcut, *conj.*, in the same way as, just as

sīdus, -eris, *n.*, a heavenly body; star; constellation

signum, -ī, *n.*, mark, sign, standard

silentium, -ī, *n.*, silence

sileō, -ēre, -uī, —, to be silent; to say nothing

similis, -e, *adj.*, + *gen., dat.*, like

simul, *adv.*, at the same time, together

sine, *prep. + abl.*, without

singulī, -ae, -a, *pl. adj.*, each one; every single; single, individual

sociō (1), unite (in an alliance)

socius, -(i)ī, *m.*, companion, comrade, partner, ally

sōleō, -ēre, -itus, to be accustomed

sollemnis, -e, *adj.*, traditional, customary

sōlum, *adv.*, only, just, merely

sōlus, -a, -um, *adj.*, alone

sonitus, -ūs, *m.*, a sound, noise

sors, -tis, *f.*, lot, fate

sospes, -itis, *adj.*, safe and sound

spargō, -ere, -sī, -sum, to scatter, strew

spatium, -iī, *n.*, expanse of ground, area, space

speciēs, -eī, *f.*, sight, appearance, look

spectāculum, -ī, *n.*, sight, spectacle, performance

spectō (1), to look at, watch

specus, -ūs, *m.*, a cave or grotto

spēs, speī, *f.*, hope, expectation

spīritus, -ūs, *m.*, breathing, breath, spirit, soul

spoliō (1), to strip of clothing or of arms; to despoil

spolium, -iī, *n.*, spoils, booty

(spons), spontis, *f.*, will, volition; **sponte mea / sua,** *etc.*, of my /one's own accord

squālor, -ōris, *m.*, dirtiness, filth, neglectful state

statim, *adv.*, immediately, at once

stātiō, -ōnis, *f.*, post, halting place; **in stātiōne,** on guard at one's post

statīuus, -a, -um, *adj.*, stationary, standing, still; *n. pl. as substantive*, halts

statua, -ae, *f.*, statue

statuō, -ere, -uī, -ūtum, to assign, place, position

statūra, -ae, *f.*, height

status, -a, -um, *adj.*, set, appointed

stimulō (1), to urge; to incite

stimulus, -ī, *m.*, goad, spur

stīpendium, -ī, *n.*, cash payment received by soldiers; a term of military service; a payment levied from a conquered people

stō, -āre, stetī, statum, to stand, to remain; *with pro,* to take sides with; to be fixed, established

stolidē, *adv.*, stupidly, brutishly

strāgēs, -is, *f.*, destruction, wreckage

strepitus, -ūs, *m.*, sound, noise, clamor, din

stringō, -ere, -nxī, -ctum, to bind fast, draw tight, tighten

studium, -ī, *n.*, zeal; devotion to a person, party, cause, etc.

stuprō (1), to violate the chastity of, defile by licentious conduct

stuprum, -ī, *n.*, dishonor, shame, illicit sexual intercourse

suādeō, -ēre, -sī, -sum, to advise, urge, advocate

sub, *prep.* + *abl.*, under, beneath; + *acc.*, directly after, in response to

subeō, -īre, -iī, -itum, to approach; to steal in on; to come over

subiectus, -a, -um, *adj.*, situated under; situated close at hand, adjacent

subinde, *adv.*, immediately or shortly thereafter

subitus, -a, -um, *adj.*, sudden

sublicius, -a, -um, *adj.*, supported by wooden piles

subrigō, -ere, -ēxī, -ectum, to raise to a more or less vertical position

subtrahō, -ere, -xī, -ctum, to draw or drag from under

succidō, -ere, -dī, -sum, to cut from below or at the base

succidō, -ere, -ī, to give way under one, collapse

Sulpicia, -ae, *f.,* mother-in-law of the consul Postumius

sulpur, -uris, *n.,* sulphur

sum, esse, fuī, to be

summa, -ae, *f.,* the whole of a thing as distinct from its parts; the totality

summum, *adv.,* at most

summus, -a, -um, *adj.,* highest, topmost, uppermost

sūmō, -ere, -mpsī, -mptum, to take up; to take on

super, *prep. + acc.,* over, above, beyond

superbus, -a, -um, *adj.,* haughty, proud

superiaciō, -ere, -ēcī, -ectum, to throw or scatter on top

superincidō, -ere, to fall from on top

superincubō, -āre, to lie on top

superne, *adv.,* above; from above

superō (1), to climb over, surpass, overcome

superstitiō, -ōnis, *f.,* religious awe or credulity; superstition

supersum, -esse, -fuī, —, to be in excess, abound, remain, survive

supplicium, -(i)ī, *n.,* punishment, reparation

suprā, *prep. + acc.,* above, superior to

sustineō, -ēre, -tinuī, -tentum, to keep erect; to support, hold up, sustain

suus, -a, -um, *poss. adj.,* his, her, its, their [own]

symphōnia, -ae, *f.,* a group of musicians; a band

T., Titus

taceō, -ēre, -uī, -itum, to be silent, say nothing

tacitus, -a, -um, *adj.,* silent

taedium, -(i)ī, *n.,* the state of being tired or weary (of) (+ gen.)

tālis, -e, *adj.,* such, of such a kind

tam, *adv.,* so; so much as

tamen, *adv.,* nevertheless

tamquam, *adv.,* as if, just as

tandem, *adv.,* at last

tangō, -ere, tetigī, tactum, to touch, come into contact with, reach

tantum, *adv.,* to such a degree; only

tantum, -ī, *n. pron.,* such a quantity; (*with partitive gen.*) so much (of)

tantus, -a, -um, *adj.,* so much, so great, of such a size

Tarpēius, -a, -um, *adj.,* name applied to the Capitoline or various of its features

tēlum, -ī, *n.,* weapon, spear

temerē, *adv.*, blindly, heedlessly, recklessly

temperō (1), to exercise restraint, restrain oneself, refrain (from)

templum, -ī, *n.*, area of sky or land marked out for taking of the auspices, temple

temptō (1), to test, try, make an attempt on

tempus, -ōris, *n.*, time, period

tenebrae, -ārum, *f. pl.*, darkness, obscurity, concealment

teneō, -ēre, -nuī, —, to hold, keep, occupy

tergum, -ī, *n.*, the back

terminus, -ī, *m.*, limit, endmost point, end

terra, -ae, *f.*, land, earth, ground

terreō, -ēre, -uī, -itum, to frighten, terrify

terror, -ōris, *m.*, fear, terror

testāmentum, -ī, *n.*, will

testor, -ārī, -ātus sum, to invoke as a witness; to affirm or declare

Tiberīnus, -ī, *m.*, of or belonging to the Tiber

Tiberis, -is, *m.*, the river Tiber

timeō, -ēre, -uī, to fear, be afraid

timidus, -a, -um, *adj.*, fearful, afraid

timor, -ōris, *m.*, fear

titubō (1), totter, stumble

tollō, -ere, sustulī, sublātum, to pick up, lift, raise; to get ride of, remove

Torquatus, -ī, *m.*, cognomen of Manlius, who killed the Gaul

torquēs, -is, *m.*, a collar of twisted metal

torreō, -ēre, -rruī, -stum, to roast, scorch, burn

torridus, -a, -um, *adj.*, dried up, shrivelled (by cold, etc.)

tot, *indecl. adj.*, so many, that many

tōtum, -īus, *n.*, the whole, entirety

tōtus, -a, -um, *adj.*, the whole of, all, entire

trādō, -ere, -didī, -ditum, to hand over/down, pass on, bequeath

trahō, -ere, -xī, -ctum, to drag, pull, draw

trānō. *See* **transnō**

transcendo, -ere, -dī, -sum, to climb across or over; to go over, across; to overstep, transgress

transeō, -īre, -īuī/-iī, -itum, to come over; to go across

transfuga, -ae, *m.(f.)*, deserter

transnō (1), to swim across

transiliō, -īre, -uī, —, to jump across or over

transitus, -ūs, *m.*, the action of crossing from one side to another

trecentī, -ae, -a, *adj.*, three hundred

trepidus, -a, -um, *adj.*, alarmed, fearful, anxious

trēs, tria, *adj. numeral*, three

tribūnal, -ālis, *n.*, tribunal
tribūnicius, -a, -um, *adj.*, of or belonging to a tribune
tribūnus, -ī, *m.*, tribune
tripudium, -iī, *n.*, a ritual dance in triple time
triumphus, -ī, *m.*, a triumphal procession; victory, triumph
trux, -ucis, *adj.*, harsh, savage, pitiless
tū, tuī, *pron.*, *sing.*, you
tueor, -ērī, tūitus (tūtus) sum, to keep safe, preserve, maintain
tum, *adv.*, then, at that moment
tumultuōsus, -a, -um, *adj.*, uproarious, tumultuous
tumultus, -ūs, *m.*, commotion, uproar; a hostile incursion
tunc, *adv.*, then
turba, -ae, *f.*, a commotion; a crowd
tūtēla, -ae, *f.*, guardianship, protection
tūtor, -ōris, *m.*, a guardian; one appointed to look after a person considered incapable of handling his or her own affairs
tūtus, -a, -um, *adj.*, safe
tuus, -a, -um, *poss. adj.*, your, yours; (*emphatic*) your own
tympanum, -ī, *n.*, drum, tambourine

uacuus, -a, -um, *adj.*, empty, clear, vacant
uādō, -ere, to advance, proceed, rush; go rapidly or purposefully

ualētūdō, -inis, *f.*, health
ualidus, -a, -um, *adj.*, powerful, robust, strong
uallēs, -is, *f.*, valley
uānus, -a, -um, *adj.*, insubstantial, empty, useless
uarius, -a, -um, *adj.*, changeable, fluctuating, inconsistent
uastus, -a, -um, *adj.*, desolate, deserted
uātēs, -is, *m.*, prophet, seer
uāticinor, -ārī, -ātus sum, to prophecy; to rave
uāticinus, -a, -um, *adj.*, prophetic
ubi/ubī, *interr., rel., and indef. adv.*, in which place; where; when
ubicumque, *rel. adv.*, in whatever place, wherever
ubique, *adv.*, and where
-ue, *enclitic conj.*, or
uelut/uelutī, *adv.*, as, just as, as if
ueneror, -ārī, -ātus sum, to worship, pay homage to, revere
uenia, -ae, *f.*, indulgence, kindness
ueniō, -īre, uēnī, uentum, to approach; to come
uenter, -tris, *m.*, belly, abdomen
uerbum, -ī, *n.*, word
uerēcundia, -ae, *f.*, restraint, modesty, diffidence
uereor, -ērī, -itus sum, to fear, be afraid, show respect for

Vergiliae, -arum, *f.,* the
constellation of the Pleides

uerō, *adv.,* certainly, indeed;
however, yet

uersicolor, -ōris, *adj.,*
variegated

uertō, -ere, -tī, -sum, to turn

uestibulum, -ī, *n.,* forecourt

uestīgium, -(i)ī, *n.,* footprint,
track, trace

uestis, -is, *f.,* clothing

ueterānus, -a, -um, *adj.,*
mature, experienced,
veteran

uetō, -āre, -uī, -itum, to forbid,
prohibit

uetus, -eris, *adj.,* old, veteran

uexātiō, -ōnis, *f,* harrassment

uexillum, -ī, *n.,* a military
standard, military banner

uia, -ae, *f.,* way, path

uīcīnitās, -ātis, *f.,* proximity,
nearness

uicis, uicis, *f.,* a recurring
occasion for action; a turn;
in uicem, in turn

uictima, -ae, *f.,* an animal
offered in sacrifice; a victim

uictor, -ōris, *m.,* victor

uictōria, -ae, *f.,* victory

uictus, -ūs, *m.,* food

uideō, -ēre, uīdī, uīsum, to see;
pass., to appear, seem

uigeō, -ēre, -uī, to be active or
lively, flourish, thrive

uigilia, -ae, *f.,* the act of
keeping watch; vigilance,
wakefulness

uīgintī, *adj.,* twenty

uīlis, -e, *adj.,* cheap

uinciō, -īre, -xī, -ctum, fasten
with bonds, to fetter, to
bind

uincō, -ere, uīcī, uictum, to
conquer, prevail, overcome,
defeat

uinculum, -ī, *n.,* bond, fetter

uindicō (1), to claim; to rescue;
to avenge

uīnum, -ī, *n.,* wine

uiolentus, -a, -um, *adj.,* violent,
savage, aggressive

uiolō (1), to violate, profane

uir, uirī, *m.,* man

uirginitās, -ātis, *f.,*
maidenhood

uirgō, -inis, *f.,* a girl of
marriageable age; a virgin

uirtūs, -ūtis, *f.,* manliness,
valour, moral excellence

uīs, uis, *f.,* physical strength,
force, violence

uīsus, -ūs, *m.,* sight,
appearance

uīta, -ae, *f.,* life, manner of life

uitium, -ī, *n.,* moral failing,
fault

uītō (1), to steer clear of, shun,
avoid

uitricus, -ī, *m.,* step-father

uīuō, -ere, -xī, -ctum, to be
alive, live, be animated,
survive

uīuus, -a, -um, *adj.,* alive, fresh

uix, *adv.,* with difficulty,
scarcely

ullus, -a, -um, *adj.,* any, any at
all

ultimus, -a, -um, *adj.,* most
distant, farthest away, end
of, remotest

ultor, -ōris, *m.,* avenger

ūltrō, *adv.,* of one's own accord;
spontaneously

ululātus, -ūs, *m.,* yelling,
howling

umbra, -ae, *f.,* shadow, shade

umquam, *adv.,* **unq-** at any
time, ever

unde, *rel. and interr. adv.,*
whence, from which place

undique, *adv.,* from all sides;
from every side

ūniuersus, -a, -um, *adj.,* the
whole of, entire, universal

unquam, *See* **umquam**

ūnus, -a, -um, *adj.,* one

ūnusquisque, ūnaquaeque,
ūnumquidque. *See* **unus,**
quisque

uocō (1), to call, invoke; to
summon

uolg-. *See* **uulg-**

uolnus. *See* **uulnus**

uolō, uelle, uoluī, to wish, want

uoltur. *See* **uultur**

uoltus. *See* **uultus**

uoluntās, -ātis, *f.,* will, wish,
intention

uōs, *pron., pl.,* you

uōtum, -ī, *n.,* vow, pledge

uoueō, -ēre, uōuī, uōtum, to
vow

uox, uōcis, *f.,* voice

urbs, urbis, *f.,* city

urgeō, -ēre, ursī, to press
upon, squeeze, thrust,
weigh down, bear hard on;
encroach on

usquam, *adv.,* in any place;
anywhere

ut, *adv. how, just as*
and *conj.,* + *indicative* as,
when, + *subjunctive* so that;
with the result that

utcumque, *adv.,* in whatever
manner or degree

uter, utra, utrum, *interr. and*
rel. adj., which of two

uterque, utraque, utrumque,
pron., each, each of two

utinam, *particle,* would that, if
only

ūtor, -ī, ūsus sum, to use, make
use of; to employ

utrimque, *adv.,* on both sides

uulgātus, -a, -um, *adj.,* public

uulgō, *adv.,* in a mass

uulgus, -ī, *n.,* the common
people, crowd

uulnus, -eris, *n.,* wound, injury

uultur, -uris, *m.,* vulture

uultus, -ūs, *m.,* facial
expression, countenance

ℬℭ LATIN Readers

Series Editor: RONNIE ANCONA, HUNTER COLLEGE

Other Readers Also Now Available

A Lucan Reader
Selections from CIVIL WAR
SUSANNA BRAUND
(2009) ISBN 978-0-86516-661-5

A Plautus Reader
Selections from Eleven Plays
JOHN HENDERSON
(2009) ISBN 978-0-86516-694-3

A Sallust Reader
Selections from BELLUM CATILINAE,
BELLUM IUGURTHINUM,
and HISTORIAE
VICTORIA E. PAGÁN
(2009) ISBN 978-0-86515-687-5

A Terence Reader
Selections from Six Plays
WILLIAM S. ANDERSON
(2009) ISBN 978-0-86515-678-3

A Roman Verse Satire Reader
*Selections from Lucilius, Horace,
Persius, and Juvenal*
CATHERINE C. KEANE
(2010) ISBN 978-0-86515-685-1

A Suetonius Reader
Selections from the LIVES OF THE
CAESARS *and the* LIFE OF HORACE
JOSIAH OSGOOD
(2010) ISBN 978-0-86515-716-2

Forthcoming in 2011 and Beyond

**An Apuleius
Reader**
ELLEN D. FINKELPEARL
ISBN 978-0-86515-714-8

A Caesar Reader
W. JEFFREY TATUM
ISBN 978-0-86515-696-7

A Cicero Reader
JAMES M. MAY
ISBN 978-0-86515-713-1

**A Latin Epic
Reader**
ALISON KEITH
ISBN 978-0-86515-686-8

A Martial Reader
CRAIG WILLIAMS
ISBN 978-0-86515-704-9

An Ovid Reader
CAROLE E. NEWLANDS
ISBN 978-0-86515-722-3

**A Propertius
Reader**
P. LOWELL BOWDITCH
ISBN 978-0-86515-723-0

**A Roman Army
Reader**
DEXTER HOYOS
ISBN 978-0-86515-715-5

**A Roman Women
Reader**
SHEILA K. DICKISON
and JUDITH P. HALLETT
ISBN 978-0-86515-662-2

A Seneca Reader
JAMES KER
ISBN 978-0-86515-758-2

A Tacitus Reader
STEVEN H. RUTLEDGE
ISBN 978-0-86515-697-4

A Tibullus Reader
PAUL ALLEN MILLER
ISBN 978-0-86515-724-7

 VISIT THE SERIES WEBSITE FOR UPDATES
ON AVAILABLE VOLUMES:
www.bolchazy.com/readers